# WEALTHY AND WHITE

# WEALTHY AND WHITE

Why Guys Like Me
Have to Show Up, Step Up,
and Give Others a Hand Up

ED MITZEN

**LIONCREST**
PUBLISHING

WEALTHY AND WHITE
*Why Guys Like Me Have to Show Up, Step Up, and Give Others a Hand Up*

FIRST EDITION

ISBN    978-1-5445-4099-3    *Hardcover*
       978-1-5445-4097-9    *Paperback*
       978-1-5445-4098-6    *Ebook*
       978-1-5445-4100-6    *Audiobook*

*To my beautiful wife Lisa, for being the person behind the elephant, with a shovel cleaning up my messes. And for her meatloaf.*

# CONTENTS

# INTRODUCTION

A few years ago, I sold my marketing business in Saratoga Springs, New York, and my wife Lisa and I found ourselves wealthier than we ever dreamed. We'd never have to work again. We could travel. We could enjoy a nice vacation home. We were both in our early fifties.

As we planned what to do in the next stage of our lives, we agreed that philanthropy needed to be a big part of it. Philanthropy had been a pillar of my former company, Fingerpaint, and Lisa and I wanted to continue to help others and build stronger communities.

The problem, if you could call it that, was that both Lisa and I are doers. I'd been a serial entrepreneur all my life, and Lisa was a natural leader, highly organized and detail-oriented. We wouldn't be content sitting back and writing checks to worthy nonprofits and watching passively as they spent the money. We knew we'd be writing checks—we'd been big supporters of the Humane Society and local nonprofits when

I was running Fingerpaint—but we wanted to roll up our sleeves and get our hands dirty.

This book is the story of what that looked like.

## WE HAD NO IDEA

We went to work with vague plans. We wanted to use our business-building skills to help others. We wanted to give people good jobs with benefits and generate profits we could donate to the causes we admired. We wanted to level the playing field for people without the same privileges and opportunities we'd had. We wanted to help the homeless. We wanted to help animals. We wanted to renew neighborhoods. Like any start-up, we wanted to try a lot of different things and see what worked and what didn't, and make adjustments along the way. Our money made it possible for us to take chances that nonprofits generally can't afford to take. We wanted to fail fast and make a big, big impact.

So we dove in head first. And in the few years since we started our nonprofit Business for Good (BFG), we learned a lot. We've learned how to run bakeries and restaurants. We've learned how to renovate old buildings. We've learned how to push projects through bureaucracies, how to listen, and how to measure our impact.

But maybe the most important thing we came to understand is that we need to inspire other wealthy white people in this country to follow the trail we've marked. Nearly $500 billion was donated to nonprofits in the US in 2021—more than ever before—yet the problems our country faces continue blowing up. The number of homeless keeps rising. The disparity between rich and poor widens. Women continue to struggle to preserve fundamental rights to equal pay and control over their bodies. Politics is a fucking shit show.

And, perhaps more significantly, the inequities between Black people and white people only worsen. The caste system in our country remains potent and desolating, embedded in every facet of our government, economy, and culture. I wouldn't say my awareness of that was acute two years ago in 2020, but I sure as hell see it now. The more people we met and the more projects we started, the more Lisa and I realized that our wealth blossomed in a one-sided society that gave us breaks while others were held down, a knee to their necks. We benefited from that unfair advantage, and as that fact dawned on us, we became even more committed to the work we were doing.

This book is written for wealthy white people like Lisa and me. We're not out to make you feel shame or guilt for your wealth. We enjoy the freedom and nice things our wealth brings. So I'm not asking you to sell everything and live a monastic life. You worked hard for your wealth; enjoy it.

But I will try to convince you to do something more with your money. I want to convince you to help others by using the entrepreneurial skills that made you rich. Invest in people. Rebuild the neglected. Listen to the hard-working people fighting for their lives and use your influence and savvy to raise them up. Rally your rich friends. Buttonhole your politicians. Put your money to work, brother. Roll up your sleeves.

Why? Good question. Do you have an obligation to give back to the society that made you rich? Andrew Carnegie, whose ideas about philanthropy inspired me, thought so. Do you want to rewrite your reputation as a fat cat propped up by a lopsided system that favors the white and wealthy? If that motivates you, go for it.

But let me give you a better reason:

It feels great.

There is no better way to spend your money. When you remodel a basement restaurant for a Black chef whose enslaved ancestors picked cotton in the hill country of South Carolina, the joy and rewards overflow. (Even when you love her fried chicken but have to pass on the collard greens.) When you donate a few hundred thousand dollars to a program that teaches inner-city kids a trade and leads them to a lucrative career, the satisfaction pours through you. When you donate a million dollars to help a downtrodden neighborhood build a new pool to replace the leaky cement pond kids swam in for a hundred years, your sense of accomplishment will overpower any business success you've ever had. When you help two aspiring black female lawyers open their private practice, the joy it will bring you is immeasurable.

## THE MODEL IS NO MODEL

This is not a how-to book. It will talk about some of the projects Lisa and I have started and the various causes we've supported, but I don't expect you to model what we've done. You might get some ideas, but frankly, we've been all over the map. We've bought businesses, made donations, given grants to struggling small business owners, put roofs on people's houses, supported humane societies, invested in homeless shelters and housing for battered women, and stocked warehouses with free sports equipment for teams in poor schools. We've built restaurants and refurbished old brownstones. We've tried everything and anything, making our work almost impossible to categorize. We're still learning our true wheelhouse.

But that's us. You likely will do it differently.

You have to find out for yourselves what's needed in your communities. That means you have to put yourself out there. You must find those quiet leaders in downtrodden communities and talk to them. You must find the courageous, disadvantaged warriors in your city and *listen* to them. You have to help the people who you know will go on to help others, compounding your investment. At every turn, you must ask yourself, *How can I help?*

I don't care what you do, only that you do something.

# CHAPTER 1

# IT'S ON US

Lisa and I put on formal wear and hopped in the car to drive to the convention center. It was a warm fall evening, and the trees along the interstate were starting to turn. My daughter Grace leaned in from the back seat as she and Lisa scrolled through the table assignments for the dinner. "Stalk scrolling," Grace called it. She'd just started working at the foundation as a writer and photographer.

BFG was two years old, and we were receiving an award from the Capital Region Chamber of Commerce for our work. Lisa and I were both a little nervous about our acceptance speeches. I would have preferred to stay home and watch *Thursday Night Football*. But speaking tonight was an opportunity I couldn't pass up.

Lisa looked great, as usual. She smiled and handed me her phone. "Can you carry this for me?" she said. She held up her purse, a small jeweled pouch. "It won't fit," she explained. I tucked it away in my tuxedo breast pocket.

Lisa spoke first that night. She thanked the chamber, thanked the BFG staff, and talked about the people we had helped. The single mom who'd launched an iced tea business. The chef whose restaurant we renovated. The former nurse we helped grow her florist shop. The building restoration business owner who hired ex-cons and helped them get re-established in society. The two female public defenders we'd help get started in private practice. They deserved the award just as much as we did, Lisa said. Then she pointed out that the work we were doing required a long-term commitment and that we needed help. We need help from you, she told the crowd. We need the people in this room.

"We need to step up," she said. "If we want to rejuvenate our cities, break down the stubborn barriers of our caste system, and allow *everyone* to be prosperous, we all need to act."

When I took the podium, I looked out over the massive hall filled with 1,200 people. It was a sea of white faces. Down in front, the BFG table was one of the exceptions. We'd invited some of the people we worked with to sit with us. Kizzy Williams, the chef, was there. So was Jamil Hood, who ran the youth basketball program, and Marie Campbell, the florist. Norma Chapman, the community organizer from the mostly Black West Hill area, sat next to Jamil. Our other table was towards the back of the hall. Jahkeen Hoke, our foundation's CEO, sat there, along with Kim and Rayshea, the attorneys, Connie Frances Avila, our CBO, and Wadler St Jean, our CFO. Another stark contrast in this ocean of whiteness.

Every wealthy or upper-middle-class businessperson from the New York Capital Region had to be in this room. There were bankers, accountants, entrepreneurs, executives, marketers, politicians, and consultants. Planners and architects. Restaurateurs and real estate developers. Corporate execs and mom-and-pop operators. And 95 percent of them were white. What should I say to these people? What was going to knock them out of their contented seats and get them looking at the world differently? Did I need to piss them off? Did I need to make them feel guilty? Or did I just need to pull them in, each one of them, and convince them to join Lisa and me?

"Two years ago, I was afraid to drive into the Black neighborhoods of Arbor Hill in downtown Albany," I said. "I'll admit it. You turn on the news, and everything you hear is bad, right? Shootings, murders, drugs, racism. You switch on the national news, and another innocent Black kid has been shot, and our former president is firing up the white supremacists into violent mobs. It can be disheartening and soul-sucking. It starts to feel hopeless. It feels like there's nothing we can do to turn the ship around.

"That's not to say people aren't trying. We have an incredibly generous community. We have over a thousand nonprofits doing God's work for the unfortunate every day. But no one is fixing the underlying issues. The nonprofits aren't. The government isn't. It's like putting a Band-Aid on a gunshot wound. The homeless shelters are still packed. The food pantries are overrun. Black people can't get loans to buy houses and fix them up.

"Who's going to fix this problem?"

I glanced down at Norma, who'd started a community center

for kids and seniors in her West Hill neighborhood. I smiled at Kizzy, who feeds kids who don't get meals at home. Kim and Ray, sitting in the back, had rebuilt a brownstone on one of the worst streets in south Albany and showed the city what two talented Black women-warrior attorneys could do. They were all doing what they could, but they needed help.

"*We* have to fix it," I said. "The business community and business leaders—everyone in this room. We're the ones who have to fix it. We control everything in the Capitol Region. We control the banks. We control the hospital system. We control the shopping malls and grocery stores, the legal system, and the construction industry. We control the schools. We control everything! We decide who gets hired, how much they get paid, and whether they'll get insurance. If we want to make lasting change, we're the ones to do it. *It's on us.*"

I told them how BFG was renovating what used to be a whites-only University Club for the Albany Black Chamber of Commerce (ABCC). When we were finished, it would be the nicest Black chamber in the country. I told them how we were renovating restaurants and donating profits to charity. We were developing plans to flip deserted buildings into affordable housing. We were investing in small businesses. We'd pledged a million dollars to rebuild the Lincoln Park Pool because the kids in South Albany deserved to have the same kind of state-of-the-art pool as the kids in Saratoga Springs and Clifton Park. I gave out my email and told them I would answer every person who wrote to me.

Me, Deshanna and Jahkeen at the new Albany Black Chamber of Commerce prior to the grand opening. (Photo Credit: Tyeisha Ford)

Announcing our commitment to rebuild the Lincoln Park Pool for the South End of Albany with Mayor Kathy Sheehan

"We need your help to keep this thing going," I said. "Remember how I mentioned that the news is all soul-sucking and depressing? It's all doom and gloom? Well, I love Arbor Hill now. I have extended family there. I'm not afraid anymore.

"And I promise you that if you jump on this train with us and get involved with what we're doing and dig into these communities and meet the people, your heart will expand, and it will be some of the most rewarding work you've ever done. We must attack these social problems with the same ferocity as we attack our own companies' business challenges. The folks we're helping aren't looking for a handout. But they could use a hand up."

Lisa and I weren't back to our seats before we were mobbed. My phone was blowing up from text messages. Lisa's phone was buzzing in my chest like a hive of bees. The waiters had delivered plates of food, but neither of us was able to get a bite. Insurance agents, casino executives, bankers, hospital CEOs, and real estate agents strode through the aisles and converged at our table. *We can help. Call me. Let's set up a meeting. There's someone I want you to meet. We've got money.*

I guess we'd said the right thing. After two years and dozens of wide-ranging investments and projects, maybe BFG was finally getting some traction.

### WHY ME AND WHY YOU

Say what you will about Andrew Carnegie—he paid his workers shit, exploited child labor, and used unethical business practices to keep prices for his steel high—he was serious about using his wealth to help others.

Carnegie had moved to Pittsburgh with his family just as the city was becoming the nation's iron and steel manufacturing epicenter. Pittsburgh was close to the ore and close to railroads, and Carnegie built the most extensive iron and steel enterprise in the world. He gobbled up competitors, partnered with railroads, proved the concept of steel bridges, lobbied Congress for favorable tariffs, and sold his empire to J.P. Morgan for over $300 million. Carnegie's end—$225 million—was the equivalent of over $7 billion by today's standards. After retiring, he began giving away as much of that fortune as he could. All told, he gave away about $350 million—somewhere in the neighborhood of $10 billion in today's dollars.

"I resolved to stop accumulating and begin the infinitely more serious and difficult task of wise distribution," Carnegie said. "Wealth is not to feed our egos but to feed the hungry and help people help themselves."

"The man who dies rich dies disgraced."

I didn't start reading about Carnegie until after Lisa and I had started BFG. But what he had to say about wealth and the wealthy's responsibility to help others hit home for me. If you're a wealthy white person, it should have the same impact on you. I don't feel guilty for making a lot of money building a great company, and neither should you. But now that you have wealth, what will you do with it? Think about it. Do you feel you owe something to the society that helped you succeed? Do you owe something to your community?

Whether you realize it or not, if you're an affluent white guy like me, you have it easier than most people. You worked hard, sure, but just the fact that you were white and male gave you a leg up on everyone. You had access to role models. You had access to money. You got through doors that were shut to others. You were protected by laws and customs, while others were *held back* by those same laws and customs.

I know what you're going to say. *I'm not ashamed of my success. I worked for it. I'm not about to feel guilty about enjoying my wealth.* I hear you, man. I hear you. And I'm not telling you to feel guilt, shame, or embarrassment. How can I do that? I've got a pilot for my private jet on salary. I enjoy the hell out of my wealth. But none of it would mean shit to me if I weren't putting my money to work helping others and building a better community in my backyard.

Last fall, I was walking through a garage where I keep a few old vehicles I've collected over the years. I have a Mustang, a 1970 Volkswagen van, and a couple of motorcycles. My pride and joy was a blue 2002 Ferrari in great condition.

But my mind was elsewhere. I'd spent the day meeting with some folks at the YWCA in Troy, New York, where scores of women who've fallen on hard times can find a place to sleep and get help making a fresh start. The Y is the area's largest housing provider for homeless single women or women with children. Some of those women have fled their abusers. Others are trying to kick a drug habit or get some of the medicine or therapy they need to survive. The staff there is helping them in every way they can with food, training, shelter, referrals—anything that will help these women get back on their feet and into the world. Some of the women stay just a few days. Some stay for months. The Y doesn't care how long they stay as long as they are safe and thriving.

The problem was that their building was starting to fall apart. For one thing, they needed a new roof. They had a beautiful old brick building in a part of downtown Troy showing signs of renewal, but the place would go fast if they had water pouring in.

So, walking through my garage that day, I started thinking. *Do I really need these cars?* I glanced down at my Ferrari. Beautiful car. But it felt a little meaningless as I thought about homeless women with young children having no place to go in the dead of winter in Troy, New York. They didn't deserve that. They didn't *choose* to be there. But who was going to fix that? Who was going to put that roof over their heads? The Y didn't have the money. The city might open a "warming station" if the temperature got below thirty-two degrees, but how fucked up is that? What, the women aren't going to suffer if it's only thirty-three degrees? The next day I got with Jah and Connie and told them I wanted to auction off the Ferrari and donate whatever we got for it to the Y. And so we did. I'd paid $90,000 for the car, but it went for $122,000. A few weeks later, we cut a check to the Y.

### WE NEED TO FIX THIS

I was home the day the truck came to pick up the Ferrari. I loved that car. Lisa and I live in the country and enjoyed tooling around those winding back roads in that sportscar. But nothing about that pleasure came close to the joy I got a few days later when we gave the money to the Y. The women who run the place—jammed into hot little offices, their desks piled high with thousand-page grant proposals along with heating bills and contractor estimates—were overjoyed. They couldn't stop grinning. They deal with a lot of sadness every day, but on that day, all they could do was throw back their heads and laugh. When we went outside to take a photo, two dozen women poured out of that building—one in a wheelchair, others holding infants—and clustered around us.

This is what I'm talking about. We need to fix things, guys. We need to see the problems and take steps to correct them. I could have written a big check to the United Way or some other noble nonprofit doing good, and next week or next month, I probably will. But meeting the women at the Y, hearing about their problems, seeing the work they do, and then taking steps to specifically help them carried so much more weight. It *meant something* to them. They'll get a new roof, but they got much more than that. Our gesture told them that their work was important. That we appreciate what they do. That we were in it with them. You can't put a price tag on that.

## IT HAS TO BE INTENTIONAL

My friend Corey Ellis talked about this recently when we gave him a tour of a building we bought in downtown Albany. It's a beautiful Colonial Revival brick building built in 1901. It's listed on the National Register of Historic Places. Andrew Carnegie once spoke there. So did William Howard Taft. The place is called the University Club, and it used to be an all-white, all-male social club for recent college grads waiting to join their fathers as captains of industry.

It's a fantastic building. Soaring ceilings, marble staircases, hardwood floors, and arched floor-to-ceiling windows overlooking Washington Avenue and Dove Street just a block from the New York State Capital. A Palladian-style window with a French door opens onto a balcony. Fireplaces here and there. There's a huge commercial kitchen, a large lounge, and a four-lane bowling alley. There are several small apartments upstairs, some with private bathrooms. Tons of office space and meeting rooms.

We bought the place for $900,000, but we had to spend $1,000,000 to renovate it and preserve its historic features. When work is done, we plan to let the new Albany Black Chamber of Commerce move in and use it for free. Our foundation also gave them $350,000 to hire new staff and expand their reach. We created a new website and membership materials for them at no cost.

The irony of the Black Chamber moving into what used to be an all-white social club isn't lost on Corey, who helped create the local Black chamber. Corey is president of Albany's Common Council, overseeing the fifteen legislative districts in the city. Before becoming president, he represented Arbor Hill, Sheridan Hollow, and Ten Broeck on the common council. He was on the first board of directors for the Albany County Land Bank, which was set up to deal with blight and abandoned buildings. I wouldn't be surprised if he's elected mayor of the city someday.

To me, it just seemed fitting to put the Black chamber in this building. There was a time when Black people couldn't set foot in it, but chamber leaders helped direct the renovation and will use it to bring the city's Black and Hispanic entre-preneurs together. They'll form partnerships, provide access to capital, deliver training, and otherwise send the message that Black entrepreneurs finally have some resources in this city. They will have a place to socialize and network.

"This building sends the message that we are here to stay and here to make a difference," Corey told me that day during a building tour. "This building legitimizes us in both the Black and white communities."

Probably twenty workers were on site, hanging wallpaper, painting, putting up drywall, replumbing, rewiring, and buff-ing marble stairs. The chamber's new CEO, hired away from the city of Atlanta after running its multimillion-dollar film and entertainment office, was on-site to map out where fur-niture should go and how offices should be configured. The work was progressing slower than I wanted, but working with the historic preservation office required that we wait for approvals on some of the details.

With the University Club, I'm hoping the Black business community can start to see some of the privileges white entrepreneurs like me usually take for granted. Black people were cheated out of the kind of generational wealth white people use to buy and build their businesses, but this new headquarters will give them a sense of pride and purpose. They'll have an elegant place to take potential clients and investors. Doors will open. Members will get word on new grant programs, news about state contracts and proposal requests, business referrals, and free publicity about their business. They'll have a voice in the state legislature.

"Perceptions are everything, and this will change how the Black chamber is perceived," Corey said. "But it's more than that."

Corey and I leaned in to hear each other over the hammers and impact drills. A couple of guys shouted instructions as they tried to move a 500-pound reception table built a hundred years ago. Suddenly it was quiet for a moment, and Corey straightened up and looked around. We were in the middle of a ballroom in the University Club. "What's important is that what you're doing here, Ed, is intentional. You're doing this specifically for *us*."

## REVISITING CARNEGIE'S MISSION

There's no record of what Andrew Carnegie said when he gave a speech to those college grads at the University Club over a hundred years ago. But I'll tell you what he's saying to *me*. He's telling me that I have an obligation to give back. I made a fortune. I worked hard for it, but I also had breaks that others were denied, and I benefited from my community and the smart people I brought in to work with me. As a result, I am responsible for giving back, spreading my good fortune, and helping people who have already started up the ladder. Carnegie built libraries, schools, and endowments to help others. I'm renovating buildings, sending business to minority entrepreneurs, and working to bring affordable housing to people who've never had a chance to buy real estate and generate the real wealth that investment brings. We're supporting humane societies and humane endeavors that create caring, thriving communities. I believe what Carnegie believed—that we have a duty to redistribute our wealth and help those who got pushed out. Giving our wealth away should take as much thought and hard work as the accumulation.

Why should you do this? Why am *I* doing this? It's not the awards. It's not the press releases and the stories in the newspaper. It's for the pure joy of helping people like Kizzy Williams, Maria Gallo, Marie Campbell, Jamil Hood, and Norma Chapman, who have spent their lives helping others without asking for anything. It's for the pleasure of seeing their eyes light up and their back straighten as the weight is lifted and the yoke is removed. I see them move more freely. Where they once saw obstacles, they now see openings. Doors are ajar. The windows are open, and fresh air blows in. The world is full of possibilities.

It's knowing, too, that I am correcting a wrong. I am returning something that has been stolen. I'm helping pick up and brush off someone who's been knocked to the ground over and over. I'm walking beside them till they regain their strength and courage and resolve and optimism.

You should do this, too. Why? Because if you are not actively solving a problem, then you are actively perpetuating the problem. This makes *you* the problem.

And I believe you need to do this work openly and publicly. When I told a buddy of mine about how my phone blew up and my inbox avalanched after my speech to the chamber, he said, "That's why rich guys donate anonymously. They don't want the parade of people with their hand out."

That's missing the point, and it's a big one. I'm doing this publicly because I want to be intentional in a way that means something to people like Corey Ellis. I want the world to know who is doing this and why. I'm doing it because there is an onus on me by dint of my wealth and my beliefs about what is right and good. I'm doing this because a lot of people got a raw deal. White guys like me have been free to run downhill while everyone else has had to trudge uphill. I'm saying, Yes, you *have* been held back. This is for you. You deserve this. You were denied—actively and purposefully—the opportunities others enjoyed, which was wrong. This is just a step in trying to make it right.

Lisa and I were exhausted as we left the convention center that night after the awards dinner. After missing the meal, I planned to have a beer and a sandwich, and Lisa was saying something about some Oreos. I thought back to when we first got started. We certainly didn't arrive at this place of honor overnight. Frankly, Lisa and I struggled at first. We had a few swings and misses before we found the sweet spot. So let's back up and tell you how we got started and overcame some of our early mistakes.

# CHAPTER 2

# FUCKING UP AT FRANK CHAPMAN

The Frank Chapman community center sits on First Street in the West Hill district, one of the worst neighborhoods in Albany. It wasn't hard to find. I just headed south from my home in Saratoga Springs and stayed on Route 9 as it narrowed, entered the city, and snaked northwest on Second Street past the condemned buildings and boarded-up houses.

Decades ago, this was a nice part of town. A few blocks south, lumber barons in Arbor Hill built beautiful brick buildings, churches, and theaters. Then, after the Great Depression, immigrants and young families moved in and added their own touches to the row houses, tree-lined streets, and parks. But most left as the suburbs sprawled and the great White Flight of the sixties emptied inner-city neighborhoods. Today, West Hill is 70 percent Black and 10 percent Hispanic.

You would not call this section of Albany prosperous. Not

by a long shot. I spotted a few grocery stores selling beer, cigarettes, and lottery tickets, but otherwise, there was very little commerce. No insurance agencies. No law offices. No repair shops or clothing stores. No Starbucks. For years, murders, rapes, and armed assaults were commonplace in West Hill. Prostitutes and crack dealers operated out of the parking lots at the corner of North Lake and Clinton avenues, and residents were afraid to go out at night. In 2008, a ten-year-old girl playing on the sidewalk just a block north of the community center was shot and killed by a stray bullet fired by a fifteen-year-old using what the newspaper called a "community gun" stashed in a backyard shed for whoever needed a weapon. The local gang was known as the "Jungle Junkies."

Although violent crime is down and the neighborhood is starting to experience some rejuvenation, its residents are still mired in poverty. Three out of every four students in nearby Arbor Hill are eligible for the free or reduced-price lunch program, and the median household income in West Hill is about half what it is for the rest of Albany. People are hurting. Most residents can't afford to buy a place, so they rent or live in subsidized housing. But income levels are so low that many have little left to buy groceries after paying rent. There are more than sixty food pantries in the region.

And this is our state capital. Less than ten blocks away, wealthy lawmakers and lobbyists stroll the marbled hallways. The Empire Plaza, a vision of Nelson Rockefeller's, built for $2 billion fifty years ago, was so massive that it created a worldwide shortage of marble. If you wanted the perfect example of the disparities in our country—the gap in wealth, the disparity in race, the massive gulf between the haves and the have-nots—you couldn't choose a better place than Albany.

As I parked my pickup truck and walked south of First Street, the irony of the situation wasn't lost on me. The United States exhibits wider wealth disparities between rich and poor than any other major developed nation, and I was the poster child. When people want to talk about the one-percenters, when they want to talk about privilege, I'm the guy they are thinking about. *I'm the guy everyone loves to hate*, I thought. *I'm the problem.* I had to chuckle. I thought, *Now's your chance to do something about that.*

## MAKING A DIFFERENCE

The meeting I was heading to had been set up by my friend John Eberle, who oversaw a local community foundation. Lisa and I supported many philanthropic causes through his foundation, and I had told him that I wanted to take more of a hands-on approach to giving. I wanted to use my business skills as well as my wealth.

So John started talking about this community center in the West Hill area of Albany. "This might be a good place for you to begin," he said. The building was in rough shape, but the center itself is valuable to that neighborhood. Kids could drop in, get coaching, and play organized basketball. They had a tiny library, and everyone has to read a book before taking the court. There are services for senior citizens. There were meals served to the poor in the area. The neighborhood was trying to rebound. On Saturdays, a community group blocked off North Lake Avenue between Clinton and First and staged Zumba dance fitness sessions. There was a "Take Back Your Street" initiative led by a local doctor and the University of Albany. "People are trying," John said. "You could be a part of that."

The building was vital, but it was also falling down. When I entered, I could see that the roof leaked. Squirrels were coming through gaps in the windows. Ivy grew through the rafters and inside the building. There was no air conditioning. No security system. No decent lighting, plumbing, or electrical. If you made it something special, my friend said, it would be a real boost—not just for the kids and the seniors, but for the whole neighborhood. It could bring a sense of pride, create some momentum for new businesses perhaps, or more investment on the part of the landlords who were letting nearby properties deteriorate.

*OK*, I thought. *That sounds like something I could sink my teeth into.*

## A SURPRISING RESPONSE

John and I shook hands with Jamil Hood, who ran the youth House of Hoops program, and Norma Chapman, a state lawmaker and the daughter of the late Frank Chapman. They gave us a quick tour of the facility. There were art classes and wellness classes. Kids were doing organized basketball drills in the gym. In the lot out back, kids had built raised garden beds and were growing vegetables they could bag up and take home with them. Posters announced free turkeys for Thanksgiving, volunteer spring clean-up events, events discouraging gun violence, and networking events for local unions that were hiring. There were reading programs and free children's books. Photos of prominent Black people—from Malcolm X and Martin Luther King to Venus Williams, Mike Tyson, Magic Johnson, and Barack Obama—lined the walls. I imagined a day when *my* portrait hung on the wall, too.

Jamil was a tall, burly guy in his early fifties. He towered over me. Word was that he'd made a living on the streets before he'd left that life and found a home at Frank Chapman. Now his first love was teaching the game of basketball to neighborhood kids. Jamil had coached his son, Jamil Jr., who'd gone on to be a college star before joining his dad to run the Hoods House of Hoops. Working with the kids, the Hoods were firm but supportive. If you messed up a drill, you had to redo it. If you flubbed a pass, no worries. Happens to everyone. The kids were focused and confident.

Everything I saw convinced me I was in the right place. We sat down, and I made my pitch.

"Here's what I'd like to do," I said. "I want to buy your building from you for a dollar, and then I want to spend about a half-million dollars doing the repairs you need around here. When they're done, you will have a beautiful facility to use."

I pointed at the windows and gestured toward the rickety seating lining the gym. "We can fix all this. We'll give you a new kitchen, a bigger kitchen so you can have more events here. We'll get air conditioning so the kids can use the gym in the summer. We'll manage the renovation, get the contractors in here, and ensure they do it right."

As I spoke, I saw Jamil and Norma give each other doubtful looks. They listened silently as I spoke and then grimaced slightly when I finished.

They were polite but firm. They did not want to sell, they said. They knew their facility needed work, but they were prepared to take on the work by themselves. They would raise the money themselves. They would hire contractors and manage the repairs. They said they were grateful for my interest, but, no, they were not interested in selling. But, yeah, thanks for stopping by.

I was stunned. This was not the enthusiastic response I was expecting. This was about the *last* thing I expected. Were they really turning down a half-million dollars in repairs?

There wasn't much more to say, so we left, and I headed back home. Truth is, I was angry. *What's wrong with these people?* I thought. *A guy walks in and offers to spend $500,000 to fix their crumbling building, and they say no? I mean, how stupid can you be?* I shook my head. I'd walked in there thinking they would be blown away by my generosity. They would be overcome with sheer gratitude. We'd shake hands, embrace, make preliminary plans to transfer the funds, and get the project managers on-site ASAP. They'd see what real money can do, what true altruism looked like. But instead, they had politely told me to go fuck myself.

I drove out of the city and headed north on the interstate back to Saratoga Springs. I started thinking about Jamil, how he'd gotten off the streets of Albany and had turned his life around. Now he was turning around the lives of a lot of young people in West Hill. I thought about Norma Chapman. She'd founded the community center in her dad's memory and had spent decades working for the community. I prided myself on being someone who likes to get things done, but these people knew how to get things done too.

Then it hit me just how big of an asshole I was. How pompous. How arrogant was it to waltz in there with my checkbook and announce my plans to rescue the institution they had created? And to expect them to fall to their knees in gratitude and hang my portrait on the wall. What an insensitive douche. I'd given no thought to all Jamil and Norma had faced over the years—the broken promises and a government that offered no help. No wonder they'd turned me down. I was just the latest in a long line of phonies they'd had to deal with over the years.

I got home and sat down with Lisa. I filled her in.

"This is going to be harder than I thought," I said. Talk about a rollercoaster. I'd gone from naive grandiosity to stunned disappointment to anger and then to complete embarrassment, all in about two hours.

We decided that if we were going to be successful philanthropists, we needed to go about it differently. We needed to build credibility with the community we were trying to help. We needed a couple of small wins to show we were serious. We needed to get to know people and find out what they needed and what they were up against. Our job wasn't to ride in on our noble steeds and write checks to great fanfare. Our job was to help in any way we could. Money was just part of what we brought to the table. We also brought our compassion, humility, and willingness to share the privilege we've enjoyed. We brought our business sense and our knack for working long and hard. We brought our connections and influence. Let's put *all* of that to work, we thought.

And that was pretty much the beginning of our foundation, BFG. When you're an entrepreneur, everything looks like a potential business, so we did what all good entrepreneurs do best: launched a start-up.

# CHAPTER 3

# BUILDING THE FOUNDATION

Lisa and I weren't new to philanthropy. In addition to the work I'd done with Fingerpaint, I served for fifteen years on Paul Newman's Double H Ranch summer camp for children with severe health issues who can't go to more mainstream camps. We bought a building and planned to raise funds to provide affordable daycare. One year we traveled to Uganda, the poorest of the poor countries in Africa, to help build a health clinic and meet with the villagers we were helping. We bought two new bloodmobiles for the Red Cross, supported Saratoga County homeless shelters, and donated to STEM programs at Syracuse University for students from underrepresented communities. We wrote checks and bought tables at fundraisers. We put on hard hats and wielded shovels at groundbreakings. I paid off student loans for my employees. Every Christmas Eve, Lisa and I served food to the homeless in Saratoga Springs.

As Lisa and I discussed our strategy to build a charitable foundation, we quickly realized that we'd need a staff. We needed people to get the word out, make connections in the neighborhoods, and vet projects to ensure they were worthwhile and sustainable. I had already started talking to the owners of a bakery—the Bread Basket Bakery in Saratoga Springs—about buying their building and helping them expand their business while donating all profits to charity. I had my eye on a few neighborhood businesses in Albany, too. Our goal was not just to find people who needed help but people who needed help and were also inclined to "pay it forward" and help others as their businesses improved.

## FINDING JAHKEEN

About this time, I read an op-ed piece in the local business journal by a young Black man from Albany. He was the chief development officer for a company trying to revitalize the South End of Albany with an apartment-retail project. His name was Jahkeen Hoke, and his essay was about racial equality. He talked about his ancestors, who had been slaves, soldiers, and police officers. His grandfather had been one of the "Original Ten"—the first Black men allowed to work for the New York state troopers. One of his relatives had served with valor in the Civil War, fighting for the 54th Massachusetts Regiment—one of the nation's first Black troops. Like all Black people at the time, though, his relative could only be counted as a volunteer and never received veteran benefits.

"The great adversity overcome by my ancestors has helped pave the way for me," Jahkeen wrote. "It has taught me to tackle challenges head-on."

And the challenges he faced were significant. Although he'd

graduated from the prestigious Morehouse College and returned to Albany to work in finance and real estate development for ten years, he said opportunities for Black people in the Capital Region were scarce. The talent was there, but the opportunities weren't. Young Black people who got job interviews were often "met with awkward stares" and didn't feel welcomed. It was even worse for Black entrepreneurs. Nobody took them seriously.

Yet here's everybody talking about diversity, equity, and inclusion. It needed to be more than an agenda item, a link on the company website. The powerful had to be willing to share their power and let people run with their "real ideas... that bring about change."

I was impressed. So I called him. "I'm looking for someone to lead a new foundation," I said. "Know anyone?"

We had coffee at the bakery. He was a big guy, too—tall, with broad shoulders. He'd been a lineman in high school and college and occasionally used football analogies to make his point. I laid out my rough ideas for the foundation. We'd buy businesses and donate profits to charity. We'd support small businesses in struggling areas, particularly minority businesses. I wanted to create opportunities for the minority entrepreneurs excluded from the local business networks. I talked about planting seeds: if one business can be successful, then more will come. Jobs will come with them, and the people in places like the South End of Albany would prosper.

Jah leaned back and smiled.

"This is what I've been talking about," he said.

"Yeah?"

"Yeah," he said. "All we do is *talk* about diversity, equity, and inclusion. But it's just talk."

"We need some action."

"Right. Less talk. More action."

Understand that as the CEO of a $500 million company, I'm used to people trying to impress me and sell me ideas. In this case, the tables were turned. Jahkeen was a reserved, thoughtful person. He knew the Black neighborhoods. He'd grown up in them. He knew the community leaders. He knew the history. He knew the politicians. He knew who got shit done and who just talked about getting shit done. I saw businesses as a way to get things jump-started in neighborhoods that were in decline. So did he.

Slowly, it dawned on me: I needed this guy. But could I get him?

## PHILANTHROPY FALLING FLAT

Jahkeen was frank about charity and giving. Philanthropy, he said, was "falling flat on its face." Poverty and inequity were not just economic issues, he said. Isolation and a lack of opportunity for minority entrepreneurs also held back these communities. There is no economic support system for women and minority businesses; they aren't getting the funding, advice, and momentum that all entrepreneurs need to succeed. They stand on the shoreline while the economic current flows past them. Very few young Black entrepreneurs have successful Black mentors they can turn to. They can't build themselves up. He said that when he goes to meetings, none of the professionals—the architects, engineers, contractors, lawyers, and accountants—are minorities.

But, if you're doing these projects like a restaurant or bakery, he explained, you can make sure you hire a Black attorney to help you close the deal, a Black construction firm to remodel the building, or a Black accountant to manage the books. Your initial investment continues to reinvest itself into the community. *That* creates resilience. All you need is that one catalytic investment—not just with money but with experience and with more resources than just capital. And if you do that three times over, there will be results. The investment is compounded. The benefits accrue at an exponential rate. Jah referred to this as "building an ecosystem."

Jahkeen could see the benefits at the ground level. He'd seen the homes, apartment buildings, and businesses in his neighborhood boarded up and abandoned, but now he could see the reverse. Investing in these forgotten streets was not just "innovative," he said. It was "provocative." When people see what you're doing, you will force a level of accountability. They'll think, *Well, they're doing it; why am I not doing it too?* They'll start asking themselves, *What more should I be doing? Can I volunteer? Can I do something besides write a check?*

Jahkeen suggested a few people to run the foundation, but it was becoming increasingly obvious to me that no one would do a better job than Jah himself. I was not trying to model how other nonprofits work; I was interested in solving problems and getting stuff done, and Jah seemed fine with the idea of building the plane after we'd already taken off. We met several times. We had coffee, and Lisa and I had him out to the farm for lunch. We talked. I could see he was still trying to wrap his head around the ideas, but each time we met, he seemed more invested in this kind of work. He slowly switched from saying, "you could do this" or "you might try that," to "when we start doing this." He took my rough ideas and fleshed them out, putting real meat on the bones.

"This could be transformative for the community," he said during one of these meetings. "No one is doing what you are proposing to do. There's no model for this."

He introduced to me this idea of "propel and protect." As the organization grew—we didn't have a name for it yet—we needed to advance the projects we were working on—propel them forward—while at the same time protecting the work we'd already invested in. We couldn't continually lunge forward while leaving last year's projects to wither on the vine. Again and again, he indicated that he had no interest in joining a check-writing or grant-making foundation. Those were fine, he said, but he kept meeting with me only because he wanted to make things happen in his hometown community. "I like to be part of the solution," he said. "I like to do the work."

"So, how do we get started?" I asked him.

"We're going to need some base hits to build up the public's trust and confidence in us," he said. "There might be a lot of suspicion about our motives, and some people might try to take advantage of us. There might be some rough patches. But if we're ready for them, we'll get past them."

Music to my ears.

I offered him the job, and he accepted.

## COMING HOME

For Black kids like Jahkeen growing up in Albany, it was understood that you left as soon as possible and never came back. There were 1,300 kids in Jahkeen's freshman class at Albany High, but only 423 would graduate on time after four years. Those are long odds, but it was even worse for Black kids. That freshman class was 70 percent African American when Jahkeen started, but four years later, only 30 percent of the graduating class was Black.

At Morehouse, Jahkeen volunteered in Atlanta communities where the business leaders and professionals who mentored him were all Black. There were Black doctors, lawyers, engineers, business owners, and accountants. He'd never seen that in Albany. One summer, he came home to work for General Electric in Schenectady. He'd run into old friends on the streets, and they'd stop and stare as Jah strode up in his white shirt and tie. *Jah, my man. What's up? You going to court? A funeral?* It had to be something like that because no one dressed for jobs the way Jahkeen was dressed. But Morehouse had taught him a few things about success, and Jah knew successful people dressed for the part.

Still, he never imagined returning to Albany to live full-time. Although Albany had been a manufacturing hub for over a hundred years, those jobs were gone. More than 5 million high-paying manufacturing jobs disappeared in Albany and the rest of the US between 2000 and 2010. Albany became part of the Rust Belt and struggled to create new jobs.

Then in 2004, the region attracted a budding high-tech, chip-making industry. About the time Jahkeen graduated, the tech industry was bringing in thousands of chip-making jobs a year. Albany joined the Brain Belt, and Jahkeen decided to join the young professionals flocking to the region to join the tech sector or related industries.

Having grown up here, Jahkeen had a different perspective than the others, though. Although jobs were plentiful, he didn't see many young people from his old neighborhood getting them. Technology was shaping the world and the Capital Region, but many people in Albany didn't see themselves as part of that resurgence. Jahkeen wondered if he could bridge that gap. How could he ferry his brothers and sisters across that divide? How could BFG help?

### RETURNING TO FRANK CHAPMAN

As a kid, Jah spent a lot of time on First Street at the Frank Chapman center, officially known as the Frank Chapman Memorial Institute. The institute was started by Norma Chapman in 1995 and is named after her father, Frank, who was the first Black baggage and ticket agent at Albany's Greyhound bus station. Frank had dedicated his life to helping low-income youngsters in Albany. He created apprenticeship programs that helped kids learn carpentry, landscaping, and construction, and when he died in 1987, Norma continued his work with the neighborhood's children. Jah knew Norma, who had retired from the state comptroller's office and had been elected to the Albany County Legislature three times.

I told Jahkeen about my failed attempt to buy the building and put some money into it.

"They didn't know you," he explained. "Plus, why would they want to work with you after you told them the thing they spent their lives building was a piece of shit?"

He talked about scar tissue and calluses. They'd been fucked over too many times not to be wary of a rich white guy who wanted to buy their building for a dollar on the promise that he'd fix it up for them. *Yeah, right.* If something sounds too good to be true, it probably is. Jah said he'd feel out the situation and see if there was another way in.

This was not a quick phone call to smooth things over. Jah had to work a bit. He dropped by Frank Chapman a couple of times to say hi to Jamil and chat with Norma. *Look how big this boy is,* Norma would say. *Wish you had that size when you played for me,* Jamil said. Jah met with Corey Ellis to see how they might help soften up Norma and Jamil, and reassure them a little. Jah would drop my name from time to time. *You know he just gave money to that group, don't you? The man's the real deal. He wants to help.*

Finally, Jah sat down with the entire Frank Chapman board.

Corey came by and talked about community investment and what that looks like. We need partners like Ed Mitzen, they said. We need to be able to hear them out, give them feedback, and create an environment where they're embraced.

Meanwhile, I had to learn patience—not one of my strengths. Jah was vague about what he was doing. "Still building the relationships," he'd say. Initially, I thought I needed to take ownership of the building so I could more effectively oversee the renovations and ensure they were done correctly. If I were going to put a few hundred thousand into a building, I'd want to see that it was money well spent. That seemed important. But the longer I sat on the sidelines, the more I realized that I'd have to back down from that. I didn't need to *own* the building. I'd just pay for the renovations. Pay for the renovations and manage the construction work.

Finally, Jah got me back to the table with Norma and Jamil.

"Forget what I said last time," I told them. "I was wrong to think I knew what you needed. I love this building. I love what you do here. I want you to be able to do it forever, and I want to help make that happen. No strings. Just tell me what you need."

We took a walk. It rains on the basketball court, they said. Squirrels are nesting inside. The heat in the summer is unbelievable. Three to four kids faint every summer on the court due to the heat. As we walked, the problems trickled out. I tried to help them picture something even more ambitious. A bigger kitchen would be great for many of the programs, wouldn't it? I said. Better lighting? New carpeting? Finally, we had a pretty good list going. New restrooms. Industrial air conditioning. A security system. A project manager for the construction firm we use joined us and pointed out other things. He looked at the foundation, the electrical. We'll need to bring that up to code, he'd say. We could make this area larger and brighter.

Work started a short time later. It took several months, but the change was miraculous.

The amazing Frank Chapman Community Center staff and families.

Today, it's still the same Frank Chapman Institute, but it's vastly improved. The kids can play in the air-conditioned gym during the summer when it's hot outside. The court doesn't flood when it rains. The facility can host larger gatherings and prepare meals easier in the new kitchen. The place looks fantastic, as good as any YMCA or private club in the area, and Jamil, Norman, and their board oversaw the work and managed the project themselves. Jamil pounded the pavement for additional donations, and when the Frank Chapman Memorial Institute celebrated its grand reopening a year later, the TV film crews were there to report on the community success story.

## THE FOUNDATION TAKES OFF

In the year after we started work on Frank Chapman, the BFG staff grew quickly. In addition to Jah, we hired Connie Frances Avila to be our chief brand officer and Wadler St Jean to be our CFO. We contracted with an attorney to ensure our businesses, grants, and professional support work don't run afoul of the law. By 2022, we had nearly twenty people working at the foundation. When you count the employees for the businesses Lisa and I have acquired and manage under BFG, we have nearly a hundred people we're responsible for.

Looking back, a lot of the key developments seem serendipitous. Jah believed that a change was needed and wrote about his concerns at the same time that Lisa and I were thinking the same thing. We just happened to find each other. Jah isn't joking when he tells people we are changing the tires on a moving vehicle. Although other foundations create entrepreneurial funds and do nontraditional giving, we haven't found any charitable foundations using our approach of buying businesses, dedicating funds to hiring well and paying well, and donating all profits to charity. No one is doing that because it's too much work. And they don't appear to be helping minority-owned businesses start, thrive, or both.

Jah fields two to three calls weekly from people curious about BFG. These people come from all walks of life, from people in the community to business leaders, elected officials, and philanthropists. Our work is so different that people have difficulty wrapping their brains around it. Yes, we make donations and make grants. But we also buy businesses and buildings and invest in them. Yes, we're a nonprofit, but we want to earn a profit to do more. We sit between a private foundation and a business incubator for minority businesses. We're here to help people grow their businesses and provide more great jobs. We're the "first money in" that compels other investors to renovate the building next door or across the street. We constantly push our white business associates to hire our foundlings. Get Kizzy to cater your event. Hire Marie to do your flowers. Need an attorney? Kim and Ray are right down the street. Work with or for the Black contractors we use to demolish decaying properties. We're trying to be the catalyst for all those businesses.

We want to propel certain things that deserve to be elevated and supported—such as a minority-owned business—while protecting what we already have, like the businesses we buy and manage or the buildings we save and renovate. We're addressing economic issues but not on a piecemeal or ad hoc basis. From an economic standpoint, certain communities have been denied the opportunity to build themselves up, and that's been the situation for 200 or 300 years. So we're chipping away at the problem with everything we do.

# CHAPTER 4

# TULSA

Like a lot of people, I'd never heard about the Tulsa Massacre of 1921 until just a few years ago, when I watched an old segment about it on *60 Minutes*. The original Bob Simon story had run in 1999, when the state of Oklahoma had commissioned a study on the incident, but I caught a replay of that show. I was blown away by the horror of it.

Over the course of two days, a white mob descended on a prosperous Black section of Tulsa, killing hundreds of people, destroying successful businesses, and leaving thousands homeless. Murdered African-Americans may have been buried in mass graves, and homes and businesses were looted and then burned to the ground. Black children hid under beds and later recounted how white men stormed their bedrooms and set the curtains on fire. White men mounted a machine gun on a rooftop to mow down fleeing Black citizens. As the smoke cleared, 9,000 Black survivors were marched off to internment camps and not allowed to rebuild their beautiful Greenwood neighborhood, once known as "The Black Wall Street."

This happened in 1921. In the United States. And no one was convicted of a single crime. No one was arrested. And all insurance claims were denied under a "riot" clause.

As I watched the show, what horrified me nearly as much was that I'd never heard anything about the slaughter before. For generations, the annihilation of Greenwood was not taught in schools or mentioned in many textbooks. Even in Oklahoma. It wasn't until 2002—eighty years after 300 Black people were killed and the thirty-five blocks of their homes and businesses were left in ashes—that the state Board of Education mandated that it be taught in K–12 schools. Before then, the topic was "optional," and many teachers avoided the subject altogether. The state senator appointed to lead a centennial commission to study the riot called it a "conspiracy of silence." That commission had recommended reparations be made to Greenwood survivors, but that got swept under the rug as well.

## SURVIVORS FIGHT FOR JUSTICE

Then in early May 2022, I read a story in *The Washington Post* about how the three remaining survivors of the massacre—Lessie Benningfield Randle, 108, Viola Fletcher, 107, and Hughes Van Ellis, 101—were still being denied compensation for what they went through. They had sued the city of Tulsa, Tulsa County, the Tulsa Chamber of Commerce, the Oklahoma National Guard, and other officials for failing to protect Greenwood from the white mob. In

2005, the US Supreme Court refused to hear a similar case for reparations after federal courts ruled that the statute of limitations had expired. *There's a statute of limitations on genocide?* I thought. *Since when?* Now the defendants in this new action by the survivors were trying to get the lawsuit dismissed.

I was outraged. Not only had these white civic leaders failed to protect the Black people in Greenwood, but they had also actively participated in the massacre, the ongoing persecution of the city's Black community, and the century-long coverup of the incident itself. City police and the county sheriff's department had deputized and armed white citizens and set them loose to murder, loot, and burn down the thirty-five blocks of the Greenwood District. The local oil company provided planes used to drop turpentine bombs on buildings. The National Guard joined the mob in shooting Black residents and looting their businesses. Black bodies were tossed in the Arkansas River and loaded onto rail cars. The city declared martial law and tried to blame the incident on the Black community. Black people could only get released from the concentration camps if a white employer sponsored them to work.

As I read more—how a grand jury had indicted Black people instead of white people, how hundreds of subsequent Black lawsuits were dismissed, how the incident was whitewashed and called a "race riot" rather than the mass murder it was—I could see how modern-day civic leaders were just continuing a century-long pattern. They were just running out the clock, waiting for the last survivors to die. Ducking responsibility. Hoping the whole thing would just go away.

What could I do? Hire a high-powered lawyer to help the court fight? I thought about a couple of different things before deciding that the best response was to give these three survivors money. We'd give the three of them a total of a million dollars they could divide among themselves and their families to use however they wanted.

I knew that some people would scoff at this gesture. What's a 107-year-old person going to do with hundreds of thousands of dollars? But that wasn't the point. The point was that these people deserved justice. They had clearly been injured, persecuted, and denied justice for a hundred years, and now they wanted some official recognition that they had been wronged. In our justice system, compensation is the only mechanism available to measure that injustice, and their government was denying them.

Beyond that, I wanted to send a message to these civic groups that were continuing to dodge their own culpability. I wanted to embarrass them. I wanted to make them feel ashamed for continuing to deny these victims the fair treatment they deserved. I wanted them to understand that this is what justice looks like. I wanted to show every wealthy white guy in America that when our government fails in its responsibilities that it's up to *us* to make amends.

### "'THE FIRE AND THE FORGOTTEN'"

The first thing I did was email *The Washington Post* reporter, DeNeen L. Brown. Her story came out on a Monday, and I emailed her the same day.

DeNeen had been a reporter at *The Washington Post* for thirty-five years. In 2021, she worked on two documentaries, one for the National Geographic Channel and another for the Public Broadcasting System. The first film, *Rise Again: Tulsa and the Red Summer,* focused on the Red Summer of 1919, when there were white attacks on Black communities in over thirty cities, including Washington, DC, Chicago, Omaha, and Elaine, Arkansas, where as many as 240 Black people died. These massacres came in the wake of a post-World War I economic slump when many white people blamed African Americans for unemployment and other social ills. These slaughters set the stage for what happened in Tulsa, the worst of this wave of terror against Black people in America. Her second film, *Tulsa: The Fire and the Forgotten,* focused more on what happened in Tulsa and the lingering trauma and loss of generational wealth that ensued.

DeNeen had a personal connection to Tulsa. She was born in Oklahoma and lived in Tulsa for a time. As a teenager, before she'd investigated what happened in Greenwood, she recalled that "the place was heavy and struck me as haunted, as though the very ground had a story to tell."

I told DeNeen in an email that I'd read her story in *The Washington Post* about the three survivors and their court battle. I said I wanted to make a donation. She immediately got me in touch with Regina Goodwin, the Oklahoma state representative whose district includes Greenwood.

"I'd like to make a donation to these families to help them financially," I told Regina. "I don't know them, but I've been moved by their story. They've clearly been wronged."

Regina Goodwin with race massacre survivor Mr. Hughes Van Ellis, 101 years old (Photo Credit: Sam Levrault and The Oklahoma Eagle)

"It's been a long fight," she said. She explained that in the latest court decision, the judge had ruled that the survivors' lawsuit could move forward. It was a small victory, but at least it was progress.

"We get to fight another day for justice," Regina said. "Not only are the survivors fighting, but descendants are fighting. Each new generation will fight with the same fervor as our ancestors."

I told her our foundation wanted to give those survivors and their families a million dollars. I also told her I wanted to fly out there with several members of the BFG staff and present the money in person and perhaps meet the three survivors in person.

"If we could meet the families briefly, that would be a great honor," I said. "We just want to shake their hands and tell them we care. We're sorry about what happened and all that they've been through in the decades since. We just hope the money eases their lives a little and lets them know that their struggle matters."

She got me in touch with Tulsa S.T.E.P.S Foundation, a non-profit set up to help the surviving families, and two weeks later, we flew to Tulsa. Regina met us at the airport.

### "BLACK TULSA IS A HAPPY CITY"

Although Greenwood in 1921 was little more than thirty-five blocks of smoldering ruins, Black Tulsans rebuilt. They did this despite the fact that all their insurance claims were denied because the insurance companies declared the massacre was a "riot" not covered by their policies.

Within five years, Greenwood was enjoying a Renaissance. Black writer W.E.B. Debois visited in 1926.

"Black Tulsa is a happy city," Debois wrote five years after the slaughter. "It has new clothes. It is young and gay and strong. Five little years ago, fire and blood and robbery leveled it to the ground. Scars are there, but the city is impudent and noisy. It believes in itself. Thank God for the grit of Black Tulsa."

Over the next twenty-five years, Greenwood continued to grow, re-establishing forty grocery stores and dozens of restaurants, bakeries, theaters, clothing stores, photo studios, car repair garages, doctors' and accountants' offices, and candy stores.

Then in the mid-sixties, Greenwood was dealt another blow, first by an economic slump and redlining, and then by the construction of a new highway system. Banks would no longer loan money to Black entrepreneurs and homebuyers, and the rebuilt sections of Greenwood fell into neglect and disrepair. According to the *Tulsa World,* city planners, calling Greenwood a ghetto, rezoned the area as industrial and put Interstate 244 right through it, essentially amputating the once prosperous neighborhood from the rest of the city. The bustling Greenwood area suffocated under the onslaught of steel, concrete, and noise as the elevated freeways and cloverleafs decimated their neighborhood. Rebuilt buildings were bulldozed and many Black people, once drawn to the thriving area to find community and start businesses, moved out. In May of 1967, a *Tulsa Tribune* headline said, "An Old Tulsa Street Is Slowly Dying; Greenwood Fades Away Before Advance of Expressway."

What happened to Greenwood in the sixties was not uncommon. The same thing happened in several major cities, including Kansas City, St. Louis, Pittsburg, Detroit, Hartford, and Shreveport; Black or Hispanic neighborhoods were cut off from the rest of the city.

## VISITING THE NEWSPAPER

After we landed and met Regina, we all piled into a shuttle for a tour. Although Lisa, who was recovering from COVID-19, couldn't be there, Jahkeen, Alexa, Wadler, Mark, Stephanie, and Justin from the BFG staff were also on the trip.

Our first stop was at the *Oklahoma Eagle,* a Black newspaper run by eight-four-year-old Jim Goodwin. Amazing man. He's also a prominent local attorney who's argued cases before the US Supreme Court and the Oklahoma Court of Criminal Appeals. He fought to uphold freedom of speech and was co-counsel in a case calling for reparations for the victims of the 1921 massacre. He and his brothers have run the paper for decades, and his uncle ran it before him. The *Eagle* was first published in 1922, taking over coverage of Greenwood after Tulsa's original Black-owned newspaper was burned down.

Regina is Jim's niece. She's also the editorial cartoonist for the paper. Jim lost his arm at age nine when he fell off a horse and was struck by a train. The first hospital refused to treat him because he was Black, but the second hospital saved his life. He told me that he continued to ride and has ridden horses his whole life.

"I can't imagine the courage it took for you to get back on a horse," I said.

"I love horses," he replied dryly. "It's trains I don't trust."

In 1966, the newspaper was one of those businesses displaced by the Interstate 244 project.

## THE DISPARITY TODAY

Today, Greenwood is a sliver of what it once was. All that remains is a block of Black-owned businesses and the Vernon Chapel AME Church, a refuge for Black people fleeing the massacre in 1921. Today it sits in the shadow of the interstate. The Tulsa Arts District next door is booming, but the former Greenwood district to the north is filled with vacant lots and empty buildings. Most Black people live in north Tulsa. Only a third own their own homes. The white people live downtown. About half own their own homes. The median white income is roughly $20,000 higher than the average Black family, according to one report.

Later that morning, we drove past the Ellis Walker Woods Memorial, where Booker T. Washington High School once stood. In 1921, this was the Red Cross triage site for massacre victims. We visited the John Hope Franklin Reconciliation Park, which opened in 2018 as a memorial to the 1921 massacre. It's a National Literary Landmark to Dr. John Hope Franklin, a Harvard historian and author born into legal segregation in Oklahoma in 1915. Park tours tell the story of Greenwood and the 1921 massacre but also describe the Great Migration of Black people to the north and the story of Native Americans on the Trail of Tears.

Touring the John Hope Franklin Reconciliation Park in Tulsa with Regina Goodwin and members of Black Theatre United (Photo Credit: Sam Levrault and The Oklahoma Eagle)

Our last stop was the Greenwood Cultural Center, a beautiful brick-and-glass structure with programs, exhibits, galleries, and education programs. The exhibits trace early Greenwood, the pioneers of Black Wall Street, and the destruction and reconstruction of the area.

The attacks were sparked when a nineteen-year-old Black man, Dick Rowland, was accused of sexually assaulting a white woman, Sarah Page, in an elevator on May 30, 1921. Rowland, a shoeshine, was riding the elevator to reach the upper floor restroom of the downtown Drexel Building that the Black people were allowed to use. Page was the elevator operator and knew Rowland well. As Rowland entered the elevator, he tripped and grabbed Page's arm. She screamed, and a nearby clothing store clerk concluded that a sexual attack had occurred. Police interviewed Page and didn't show much interest in pursuing the matter further. But then the afternoon paper, the *Tulsa Tribune*, came out with an enflamed story with the headline: "Nab Negro for Attacking Girl in Elevator." Police arrested Rowland the next morning.

According to the commission that studied the incident years later, "For all the crimes that African American men would be accused of in early twentieth-century America, none seemed to bring a white lynch mob together faster than an accusation of the rape, or attempted rape, of a white woman." Hundreds of armed white men gathered outside the courthouse where Rowland was held, and a group of armed Black men, most veterans of the recently ended World War, arrived to prevent a lynching. After a shot was fired, the white mob chased the Black men to Greenwood. The devastating slaughter ensued, with deputized citizens, National Guardsmen, Tulsa police, and young boys gunning down Black people wherever they could find them.

Rowland was later exonerated, and charges against him were dropped. But a white grand jury blamed the Black men for the riots. No white man was ever charged with a crime for the riots.

## MEETING THE SURVIVORS

Just after noon, we met with the three Greenwood survivors and had a private lunch with them. Viola Fletcher, the oldest of the three at 108, spoke in a clear, crisp, unwavering voice. If you closed your eyes, you would think you were listening to someone in their thirties or forties. She had been a riveter in an aviation factory during World War II. Lessie Randle, some months younger than Viola, spoke with a gentle Southern accent and wore an elegant black hat. Hughes Van Ellis, 101, Viola's younger brother, had a warm but forceful voice and wore a US Army ball cap. He'd served in Italy during World War II. He'd earned a Medal of Honor during the war but never received it because he was Black. All their children, who are in their seventies, and grandchildren, were there. As Mr. Ellis shook my hand, he said, "I have dreamed of this day my whole life."

"We're not trying to be white saviors," I told them. "We're not trying to get on a political grandstand. But you were wronged, and we're in a position to help make your lives a little bit better. You've earned it. Spend this money however you please."

After presenting the check to the three survivors, we held a press conference. DeNeen L. Brown joined us virtually, and Ike Howard, Viola's grandson, spoke for the three survivors. He said the three shared a vision for the future of Greenwood. They wanted to see more opportunities for Black people in Tulsa. They wanted the hospital in north Tulsa to be rebuilt. They wanted more economic development in the area of Greenwood that was cut off by the highway.

"They're very smart people," Ike said of the three elders. "They're realists. They understand we need to collectively come together and do the right thing."

The media wanted to know what my motivation was. I explained that I'd read DeNeen's article and had grown angry and frustrated that the three survivors were struggling merely to have their case *heard* in court. Just a few days before leaving for Tulsa, there had been a mass shooting by a white supremacist in Buffalo, just a few hours away from where we lived. It made me feel intensely angry and so discouraged that things may never get better.

"Then I was reminded of these three amazing people who have never given up," I said. "We just hope this gift will inspire others to step up the way we have."

One reporter asked if I considered my donations to be reparations for how the survivors suffered during the massacre and in its aftermath. I made it clear that it wasn't reparations. In fact, I hate the word reparations. All it does is inflame the conversation. This was a gift to some courageous people who were being wrongly disregarded by their government. The government is ignoring its responsibility by trying to run the clock out on these three wonderful people. They deserved better.

Regina Goodwin also addressed the issue of reparations.

"We are very clear there's a difference between generosity and justice," she said. "What you see here today is generosity. Don't confuse the two issues.

"The 101-year fight is ongoing, but today this has nothing to do with reparations. This has to do with a man's heart. Today, we've experienced generosity."

Meeting with the race massacres survivors at The Oklahoma Eagle headquarters (Photo Credit: Sam Levrault and The Oklahoma Eagle)

## WHAT TULSA TAUGHT US

We flew home later that afternoon. One by one, each of the five African-Americans on the foundation staff who'd traveled with me that day stopped by to thank me. I thanked *them*. We were all emotionally exhausted.

It was easy to feel disheartened—not just by what happened in Tulsa a hundred years ago but by what is happening to this day. There has been no justice for what happened that early May morning in 1921. The city and state could easily make restitution. Admit the horror and accept the responsibility. The cost would amount to a rounding-up error in the state budget, for God's sake, but the healing would be immeasurable. Instead, state and local officials choose to ignore it. They throw up their hands and say the time has passed, the statute of limitations has run out, we wouldn't know how to fairly disburse the money.

Bullshit.

At the same time, it's easy to draw inspiration from what we saw in Tulsa. The African Americans who have experienced that horror live on, patiently making their case and calmly providing a reminder that the past can't be forgotten. Even at 108, they were looking to the future, dreaming of their community being restored. Hanging on. Stating their case. Showing their children, grandchildren, and great-grandchildren what pride and persistence look like. I thought about the work we were doing in Albany, trying to help minority-owned businesses get on their feet and thrive. Greenwood before the massacre had been a flourishing community, strong with powerful bonds. People who lived there felt a sense of community. They had a sense of pride. Wealth was possible. Security was possible. Trust. A sense of hope for the future.

Sure, we gave Viola, Lessie, and Hughes a million dollars. But they've given us so much more.

# CHAPTER 5

# BUILDING AN ECOSYSTEM

As tragic as its history is, Greenwood stands as an example of what's possible. In just two generations after the end of the Civil War, the 100,000 Black residents of Greenwood built a rich, buzzing community. They constructed all-Black churches and schools, bought and sold real estate in all-Black neighborhoods, hired Black builders and shopped in Black-owned grocery stores and tailoring shops. They went to the movies, entering through the front door and sitting in the ground-floor seats—not in the balconies the way they did in the Jim Crow South. They hired Black attorneys and visited Black doctors. Oklahoma's harsh Jim Crow laws prevented them from shopping in the white part of Tulsa, but Greenwood residents saw no need to.

The Black entrepreneurs in Greenwood had a network. They could borrow money, make connections, hire professionals, and get hired in return. They could invest and find investors. They could make referrals and get referrals. They could meet for cocktails with other business leaders and exchange tips and share ideas.

Jah calls it an ecosystem, and most Black entrepreneurs in my part of the country don't have a network like that. The tips and referrals don't come their way. Sometimes they're shut out of the white community by prejudice, but often it's just that they don't have the connections or friendships. They don't have the social equity that comes from years of back and forth of business referrals and informal partnerships. Black entrepreneurs don't get to move in those circles.

We set out to try and change that.

One morning Jah met me at the Bread Basket Bakery. He walked in with a Black woman with long hair and a confident smile. Her name, Kimberly Wallace. She was working as a public defender but wanted to join another Black female lawyer to start their own private practice. Her friend Raysheea Turner had just left the public defender's office to start their firm. The two were working remotely but hoped to open a legal practice in downtown Albany. In fact, she and Jah had already purchased an old brownstone building at 134 Central Avenue in Albany that was the former law office of prominent African-American civil rights attorney Peter Pryor. The building had been abandoned long ago and was in one of the toughest areas of downtown Albany, but Jah had made a successful offer to buy it from the local land bank.

Now they were looking at an expensive renovation to bring the place up to code, return the place to its former glory, and create a place where Kim and Ray could hang out their shingle. It was a big step with an element of risk. Could they get the building renovated? Could they get enough clients through the door? Would their project convince others to move into other nearby abandoned buildings and bring life back to that part of Albany? Their future depended on all of those things.

Kim spoke with a light, almost musical lilt to her voice. She'd been raised in Jamaica and had studied at Russell Sage College in Albany and Florida State University Law School. "I was that talkative child who asked all the questions," she said. "My family would always say, 'This one's going to be the lawyer in the family.' Turns out I was."

She'd met Raysheea, who'd majored in theater and dance before going to law school at Western New England, at a fundraising event at the Albany Capital Center. Although they were both public defenders, Kim worked in Albany and Ray worked in Schenectady and they hadn't met before. They hit it off immediately. "We're going to open a law firm together," Ray told Kim at the end of the night.

That morning at the Bread Basket, Kim talked about the odds stacked against her and Raysheea. Although they'd been able to acquire the building at 134 Central for a song, renovations were going to be staggering, and none of the banks would loan them money. Raysheea had left the public defender's office and started the practice, but Kim was still working in Albany. The two were drumming up clients so Kim could afford to join Ray in Albany. Moreover, there wasn't much in the way of support from other Black lawyers; nationally, just 5 percent of the 1.3 million lawyers in the US were Black, and just a tiny fraction was female *and* Black. If they could get their office opened and operating, they would be the first law firm in the Capital Region owned and operated by two Black women.

But they were motivated. They hadn't grown up with many Black professionals in their lives—none of Kim's professors in college had been Black, and in court, she was often mistaken as a defendant or a family member, not the attorney—but that did not intimidate them.

"We want to show that becoming a lawyer and starting your own law firm is attainable for girls who look like us," Kim said that morning.

## THE GIRL BOSSES

A few days later, I invited Kim, Ray, and Jah out to the farm for lunch with me and Lisa. Raysheea brought her son Cam. She had a broad smile and a quick, hearty laugh. She exuded confidence. At work, her name plate read "Girl Boss." She was raised in Brooklyn and had attended Russell Sage in Troy. She worked for a time as a performer with the New York State Theatre Institute before going to law school. Both she and Kim had worked in restaurants—Ray in her family's seafood restaurant in Brooklyn and Kim in her family's Caribbean restaurant on Washington Avenue in Albany. They were used to hard work. "Growing up in Brooklyn, my mother made it pretty clear that if I was going to succeed in this world as a Black woman, I would have to work twice as hard to get half as much," Ray told me.

Although their practice was still in its fledgling stages, I was impressed by how involved they were in the community. Ray is the board chair for Destine Prep Charter School in Schenectady and is on the board of Miracle on Craig Street, a grassroots collective in Schenectady focused on health and wellness through physical activity, food and farming, and personal development. She is also on the board of The Center for Community Justice, which helps low-income people find affordable or free legal services and collaborates with judges, district attorneys, and probation and parole officials to keep low-level offenders out of jail and contributing to society. Kim, meanwhile, volunteers for the local Focused Investment Review Committee, the United Way, and 4th Family Inc., which introduces underserved children to STEM programs and mentors and uses a science-based approach employing sports as a way to "switch on the overlooked aptitude" of at-risk youth. Jah started that organization.

"We focus our energy on groups dedicated to getting kids off the streets, getting their heads in books, and making sure they get a good education," Ray told me. "We want to be active in the change we seek."

The two partners seemed to have their practice dialed in from a business standpoint. They focused on real estate transactions, estate planning, personal injury, and corporate formations. They worked with a lot of entrepreneurs and start-ups. They helped get minority-owned businesses up and running. They helped first-time minority buyers get homes. The pandemic helped them go paperless and remain flexible; they met their clients in their homes and signed contracts on the hoods of cars and picnic tables. Ray managed the IT, and Kim managed the day-to-day operations. Ray, the former actor, was the more outgoing of the two. "I've learned that personality and the ability to perform are key in the legal profession," she said. Both are members of the Capital District Black & Hispanic Bar Association, the New York Women's Bar Association, and the New York Bar Association.

They were well on their way to building the network they needed, but they faced significant hurdles. The partners had office spaces, but they were separated from each other and had no common space or reception areas to greet clients. Renovating their building on Central was likely to cost several hundred thousand dollars. Neither of them had any family wealth they could tap. They were living hand to mouth.

## THE LAUNCH PAD

Lisa and I saw that Ray and Kim were neither bashful nor discouraged. They were determined. "Lawyers are Black. Lawyers are women. Lawyers are immigrants," Kim told us. "Lawyers come in all different shapes and sizes, and we're going to dominate the space and command that respect."

Lisa and I had no doubt that they would thrive if they got a leg up. So at the kitchen table, we made our pitch:

"We're going to help you get your law practice off the ground," I said. "We'll give you $200,000, so Kim can quit her public defender job and start working full-time with Ray on building your new business."

I wasn't through. "We're going to pay for all the renovations for the building. If you'd like, we'll also build you a new website and get a marketing campaign going. We'll provide all the computer and office equipment you need for your new office. And, if it's alright with you, I'd like to introduce you to some of my friends in the business community who routinely need the kind of legal help you provide."

I'm pretty sure they expected us to help, but I'm equally sure they didn't expect to hear everything they were hearing. They glanced at each other disbelievingly.

"Listen, I can't help you be better lawyers," I said. "I don't know how to practice law. But I know a lot of old white guys who are very successful lawyers, and I've talked with them and they want to help, too. They can send work your way. They can advise you. Let us help you."

Ray and Kim were not sure about taking advice from old white guys, but that was not a condition of our offer. They could take it or leave it. "They don't see your new practice as a threat," I told Ray and Kim. "They see it as long overdue and want to help. These guys have done it. They can tell you when to bring on a new partner or hire a paralegal. They just want to mentor you."

That was late 2020. Over the next eighteen months, we put more than $600,000 into the renovations. Our accountant helped them set up their books and analyzed their billing rates to ensure they were charging enough. We hired them to handle our foundation closings and employment contracts. I reached out through my network, let my contacts know that Kim and Ray do great work, and sent clients their way. To corporations that talked about diversity and inclusions, we asked them to put their money where their mouths are and hire Ray and Kim. It requires a leap of faith for these companies to take on unproven talent, but I told them, "Hey, let's help these women cut their teeth. Let's get them entrenched in our network. When your in-house counsel needs outside help, bring in Ray and Kim."

By mid-2022, Ray and Kim were cutting the ribbon across the new front door of their office at 134 Central Street. They've already hired their first associate attorney and have brought on two paralegals to handle the business coming in. A TV station covered their grand opening. The newspapers wrote articles.

"Attorney Pryor had a legacy that he left behind," Raysheea said at the ribbon-cutting. "Now we get to go in and be our own trailblazers, leave our own legacy that can hopefully transcend generations to come."

Kimberley Wallace and Raysheea Turner of Wallace Turner Law (Photo Credit: Tyeisha Ford)

"We want to help everyone, single entrepreneurs, medium-size businesses, million-dollar businesses," Kim told the gathered crowd. "We want to be successful but we also want our community to be successful!"

Having that kind of coverage served our critical goal: to show the city that this run-down section of town is coming back, that it's safe for other businesses to move in and reclaim these old buildings and bring commerce back to a street that was once bustling. We want other young professionals to see this—accountants, architects, storekeepers, restaurateurs, white *and* Black—and know that this is possible. We want nearby residents and landlords to take notice and invest. We want children walking to school to see young professionals going to work on their street. We want those children to see people who look like them and to know that they can succeed like Ray and Kim succeed.

## ALLIE B'S COZY KITCHEN

Kizzy's place is a tiny basement restaurant on Clinton Avenue just west of Arbor Hill in a rough part of Albany. Walking fast, you might go right past the place without noticing. But if Kizzy Williams is in the kitchen, you can't help but notice. The aroma fills the street. Fried chicken, fish, and shrimp. Collard greens. Cornbread, steamed mussels, and barbecued pork ribs. The best macaroni and cheese north of the Carolinas. Even in the winter, when snow blankets the sidewalks, Kizzy's barbecue is going out back, sizzling with ribs and chicken. The restaurant's name and all the recipes come from Kizzy's mom, Allie B.

Allie B was born in Bennisville, South Carolina, on the Great Pee Dee River, ten miles from the North Carolina border as the crow flies. The planters grow upland cotton there—the short fiber cotton they use to make flannel and denim—and for decades, they relied on enslaved African-Americans to bring in the crop. Kizzy's ancestors worked those fields and lived off the land, hunting squirrels, wild boars, and rabbits. They made dishes with turtle meat and raccoon. When her family moved into the projects in Harlem, they brought their recipes with them and cooked with venison and whatever exotic meats they could find there. They often sold their food on the streets of Harlem. Kizzy started doing that kind of work when she was five years old.

"Growing up, I was so ashamed of these wonderful dishes," Kizzy told me once. "But it was our culture. It was soul food. We fed each other and loved each other, and that's what made you great."

Every Memorial Day, July 4th, and Labor Day, Allie B cooked enough food for 200 people in the projects. Her dad would come through the line like everyone else. "I only get one plate?" he'd say with a smile, surveying the tables of fried chicken and fish, okra, collard greens, macaroni salad, potato salad, candied yams, and steamed shrimps. "Only one?"

"Just the one," Allie B would say. "Now help me fill up these pitchers with iced tea."

The first time I met Kizzy was the night we handed her a check to help her grow her business. She stared at it in disbelief. Kizzy's aunt asked, "That check real?" I don't think

Kizzy truly believed it was real until she deposited it the next day.

It was real.

## A FINANCIAL CUSHION

Jahkeen had identified Kizzy as one of the Black entrepreneurs in Albany who might benefit from a little assistance. Her restaurant was a neighborhood institution, but Kizzy was running it on a shoestring. Her equipment and furnishings were old, and her landlord hadn't done much to keep the place looking nice. Kizzy did a brisk takeout business, but she was open only for as long as the groceries she'd bought that morning lasted. If she was open, you were lucky. If you got there late, well, maybe next time. When she first opened, her goal was to make $100 a day. We felt she could do much better if she had a financial cushion that allowed her to expand a little, keep regular hours, and take on more catering jobs, which we felt we could funnel to her.

We were clear that none of this was our expectation. It wasn't a condition of the grant we gave her. Our intention was just to give her a little relief. Before the restaurant, Kizzy worked as a housekeeper for eight dollars an hour. She used an income tax refund to start Allie B's, and she'd built it into something wonderful. People who had fallen on hard times could stop by and still get something to eat, even if they couldn't pay. We didn't want to mess with that, but we made it clear that if she wanted help, we'd be there for her.

"We believe in what you're doing, Kizzy," I told her that day.

"This money is to help you pay for things that may have been out of your reach."

Her hands trembled slightly as she held the check and looked at the number on it. She began to cry. "All my life, I've been taking care of others, and no one has ever really been able to look out for me," she said.

I also explained that we could help in other ways. Restaurant experts Jasper and Beth Alexander were now on our staff at BFG and were available to help Kizzy in any way they could. They could help with ordering, planning, sales, and bookkeeping—all the nonkitchen work that goes into running a restaurant and makes it such a time-consuming process. I said we could help her with marketing and branding. We could rebuild her website, if she wanted, and design a new logo if she wanted. "We do not intend to take over your business or take it somewhere you don't want to go," I told her. "This is your baby. What are your goals? Is it to help the community? Is it to get rich? Is it to create a legacy to pass on to your children? Is it your dream to have a bigger, sit-down restaurant?"

"I'll take it all!" she said with a laugh. "I'll take every bit of advice you can give me."

A few days later, we met Kizzy at the restaurant to discuss her goals and what we could do for her. She cooked lunch for us. The food was fantastic. Best ribs I'd ever tasted. The cornbread alone was worth the price of a full meal. Jasper and I exchanged glances. Jasper has worked all over the world in the finest restaurants, and he wore a deeply satisfied grin. This woman could cook. If the food had been subpar, we might have said, "Here's the $40,000 and a new logo," but this food was something special. We watched as a steady stream of customers came in to pick up their barbecue pork and turkey wing sandwiches (six bucks each!) and their orders of sweet potato fries and rice and beans.

But it was more than the food. Kizzy is forty-three years old, but when she steps into her tiny kitchen and wraps a scarf around her head, she's suddenly everyone's mother, grandmother, or aunt. "I'm not too many people's sister," she said. "But people come in and call me Mom all the time. I answer to it." Kizzy introduced us to her wife and her children, and we immediately became part of her family.

Kizzy Williams, one of the most inspirational women I've ever met (Photo Credit: Tyeisha Ford)

"Allie B's is a restaurant, but it's more like a home," Kizzy told me one Sunday after I'd gone to her church with her. "People feel welcome there. When you eat there, you find your family. You find the love part. Whoever goes there will find something that belongs to them.

"Success comes from what you put in. That's Allie B's. It creates success and families and beauty in the community. When we first opened, we had drug dealers in front. No more. They respect Allie B's and go somewhere else. People who use drugs still come to the restaurant, and we feed them. They call me their mother. I have people come in who don't look like the world expects a person to look, and they call me their aunt. I have thousands of nieces and nephews."

## "STOP THANKING ME!"

Kizzy agreed to let us do some renovations on her place. We put in new floors, air conditioning, new counters, a grease trap, and a new bathroom. We replaced some old equipment. We created more room for people to sit down. We redid her sign. We surprised her with a catering truck that allows her to take on bigger jobs.

She hugged me when she saw it. In fact, every time she sees me, she gives me a big hug. I've had to tell her, "Kizzy, you've got to stop thanking me! I appreciate it, but you know this is fun for me, too, right?"

After my ham-fisted first meeting with the folks at the Frank Chapman center, I felt I was starting to learn how to do this kind of work the right way. I had been used to leading and showing people the way, but now I was letting them take the lead. I was following. Jasper and I could see the great potential in Allie B's, but we could also see the value of letting things unfold at their own pace.

Hanging with the always smiling Kizzy Williams at Allie B's Cozy Kitchen (Photo Credit: Tyeisha Ford)

Kizzy also strengthened our conviction that we wanted to work with others like her, people with the work ethic, emotional acuity, and perseverance to be more successful than they think they can be. These people are grateful for our help but also have an innate drive to help others and disburse their good fortune. Like us, they feel great satisfaction in helping others. They're generous, even if what they have to give is modest. Most were already doing this good when we showed up. With Kizzy and others, we emphasize that when we give them money, it is for *them* and not for other people they want to help. "This money is for you," I tell them. "Don't give it away. Invest in yourself. It's okay to be a bit selfish because you'll be able to make more down the road, and you can help more in the community that way."

We look for businesses that can plug into this fledgling ecosystem and help support other businesses. Say Kizzy's restaurant grows. She's going to need meat and produce distributors. She will need an insurance agent, a bookkeeper, or a commercial real estate agent if she wants to open a second location. She creates a need and an opportunity for others like her who haven't had those opportunities before. The ecosystem expands and becomes more intricate. Then maybe a bank sees the value in opening a branch, and we can get people saving and earning interest instead of losing money to predatory payday lenders. And maybe the bank sees opportunities, and now you have even more investment. Distributors see opportunities and start scheduling routes into these neighborhoods, and people like Kizzy aren't driving sixty miles a day to buy supplies. She's got time now to do those bigger catering jobs at the Capitol, which is right down the street and has a moral imperative to give her some of that business. This is how you build the ecosystem.

And entrepreneurs like me have their part to play in all this. We know how to start businesses and make them successful. And when we're unencumbered by the need to turn a profit, our success is even greater. We can inspire people, mentor people, send them business, and give others the money they need to get over the hump to where they can establish their lines of credit and don't need us anymore.

It doesn't have to be a restaurant, either. It can be a laundromat, or a landscaping business. Modernize the equipment, negotiate better rents, and lower costs for people in the neighborhood who just need a clean, convenient place to wash their clothes or need someone to beautify the weed-choked lot next to their house. It's a pretty simple equation for rich people: Help build something and then let someone else take over and earn the profit or keep it for yourself and turn the profit over to charity. You get to use what you know and what you've done a thousand times, but the reward this time is far greater than in the past because *you're helping people*.

## PICKING YOUR SPOTS

We understand that we can't help everyone. We have to turn some people away. One woman came to us with plans to open a wine and cigar bar, but she had no experience with running a restaurant or a bar and we had to say no. I hope she's successful as hell, but we have to pick our spots. We must have the highest degree of confidence that with our help and their own hard work, they can actually succeed.

I felt that way about Maria Gallo. She's a single mom who was launching a successful iced tea business when COVID-19 hit and her bottler shut down. She was driving for a food delivery service when I got a business proposal from her. All she needed was a little help, and we gave it to her. Now she's got her own boutique bottling operation going in a space down the street from Kizzy's, and her product—homemade iced tea she learned to make from her grandmother—is back on the shelves. We knew Maria would be a success and that she would pass along her good fortune to others when that success arrived.

We felt the same way about Kizzy. This is a woman who's lived in a homeless shelter. She has relatives who were sent to prison. Her mother grew up and fled the Jim Crow South and joined the great Black migration for a better life in the North. Despite all these obstacles, Kizzy achieved what she considered to be success by opening a restaurant, making a hundred dollars a day.

That's success. And we are telling her, *Let's build on that and let's get you to a thousand dollars a day so you can employ more people and hand out scholarships and show the young Black girls in your neighborhood that an African-American woman can be a successful restaurateur. Let's help you get to where you can do all the things that you want to be able to do in your heart but haven't been able to afford.* It's the same with Ray and Kim. *How do we get you out of those $60,000-a-year public defender jobs and help you start your own practice making $150,000 a year and inspiring other people like you to go to law school or medical school or business school and become a great success like you?*

## SPREADING PROSPERITY

It's working. Allie B's receipts some days top $3,000. Kizzy sends out boxed ingredients and gets on Zoom to show her customers how to cook meals. She delivers healthy meals—"Just like Michele Obama wanted," she says—to school children. She has a senior citizen's program every Tuesday, and she's working to get the contract for Meals on Wheels. She cooks all of it. She plans to open an outdoor market on a nearby lot she bought and is signing up vendors to start their own businesses in the booths she'll create there. She's planted an orchard on another lot with apple trees, peach trees, and a plum tree. The community will care for it and pick the fruit for free. She says the orchard is something she's dreamt of her whole life.

One summer day I dropped in, and she took me out to Clinton Avenue.

"People used to get shot here on Clinton Avenue all the time, but now families are starting to buy these abandoned houses," she said, nodding at a few buildings on the street. "We're starting to feel physical change. Now that there's no drugs or crime, people want to live here again."

Then she turned to me. "You and Jahkeen and Lisa, you have touched this place with your heart," she said. "We're changing history here."

And then, of course, she threw open her arms and hugged me.

# CHAPTER 6

# PROFITS TO CHARITY

It's not unusual when you tell people that you're from Saratoga Springs that their faces light up, and they say simply, "Hattie's! Best Southern-fried chicken in the world!" That happened to Lisa and me when we visited Alcatraz Island in San Francisco Bay and our tour guide asked where we lived. When we told him, he said, "Home of Hattie's! I love Hattie's!"

We had to agree. We love it too. But we're biased; we own the place.

Hattie's holds a special place in Saratoga history. Hattie Gray, a Black woman from New Orleans, opened her eponymous restaurant on Federal Street in 1938 as Hattie's Chicken Shack. She used the thirty-three dollars she saved as a domestic worker to buy the first stove and ice box, and she kept the place open twenty-four hours a day, catering to the clients visiting the nearby gambling halls, speakeasies, and jazz clubs on Congress Street. The West Side at the time was racially mixed, home to the area's African-American, Irish, and Italian families. It was also a little wild. "Saratoga is fast, man," Hattie recalled fifty years later. "It was real fast. It was up all night long."

Ms. Hattie Moseley Austin, the founder of Hattie's Chicken Shack. In the words of Hattie herself: "My goal isn't to be famous—or to make a profit—my goal is to help whoever I can." In her honor, Hattie's now donates all of its profit to charity. (Photo Credit: Michael Noonan)

So was Hattie's restaurant. She was open when the patrons left the jazz clubs, and she was open when the musicians got off work an hour or two later. She was open for the grooms heading out to the track before dawn. She was open for the white bank presidents at lunch. She was open even if you had no money; if you were hungry, Hattie would feed you. Everybody loved Hattie's and everyone loved Hattie. When a longtime customer died, Hattie showed up at the family home with a ham. When an employee showed up drenched from an unexpected downpour, Hattie would find him a dry shirt.

"Everybody in the community felt comfortable there," said one bank CEO years later. "You would go there, cheek to jowl, sit down, and enjoy some good fried chicken and be treated the same. Everybody had a good time."

In Saratoga Springs, Hattie's represented more than just great Southern food. It was a social good as well. Everyone was equal, everyone was welcome. It gave the neighborhood a wonderful charm and a sense of character and community. Hattie just wanted to help people.

Like many businesses we run through our foundation, Hattie's came to us in a roundabout way. Not long after starting BFG, we bought an old building in downtown Albany that was the former home of a restaurant called Lombardo's. Lombardo's had been a landmark in the lower Madison Avenue area since it opened in 1919 in an area of Albany known as Little Italy. Politicians from the nearby Capitol were regulars. But the building and neighborhood had fallen on hard times. Not long after Lombardo's closed, the neighborhood McDonald's also closed, and neighborhood leaders saw it as a general sign of the South End's decline. When we bought the building in 2021, our plan was to renovate it, bring in a new restaurant, draw more people to that part of town, and raise money for charity.

I wanted to make it a Hattie's restaurant.

Our plan for Lombardo's was just one of several investments we've made in dining establishments. One of our first ventures was buying a bakery in Saratoga Springs, but in the next several months, we also invested in Allie B's, Maria Gallo's iced tea bottling business on Pine Street, and then a restaurant and small cafe in downtown Voorheesville.

Why would a nonprofit get into the restaurant business? The places we bought and the ones we plan to build are social centers, places that give a street character and can magnetize a neighborhood, creating opportunities for entrepreneurs interested in opening bookstores, tailor shops, gift emporiums, sporting goods stores, furniture stores, and professional offices. Restaurants draw people to an area, and the good ones can define an area's culture and history. They can create a hustle and bustle, the way Lombardo's did in the fifties and Hattie's had since 1938. They are a vital part of the ecosystem we were trying to build in the Capitol region.

Even though it had been closed for several years, when I walked into the abandoned Lombardo's building in 2021, I could feel the history and picture the neighborhood families, business people, and politicians who had visited the place for generations. The neon sign was still on the outside, and the place still had its original tiled floors, kitchen, tin ceiling, and rich wooden tables and booths. It evoked a more vibrant and exciting time. The walls were covered with murals commissioned about the time Prohibition ended. All I could think was that a Hattie's restaurant would be perfect for this location.

## GETTING JASPER AND BETH

So I did what I do: I bought the building and called Jasper and Beth Alexander, the owners of Hattie's, to see if they might consider expanding to the old Lombardo's site.

"I'd like to open a Hattie's and donate all profits to charity," I told Beth that day. "I think it's a great idea, but I'm not sure what's in it for you."

She laughed. Jasper was off skiing, so she said she'd talk it over with him and get back.

I didn't know the Alexanders well but knew a little about their history. They were living in Seattle when Beth learned in 1998 that Hattie's was for sale. She'd worked at the Chicken Shack when she was younger, and she and Jasper had met in Saratoga Springs while working summer jobs. Jasper had gone on to attend the Culinary Institute of America in Hyde Park, New York, and was making a name for himself in the booming culinary scene in the Pacific Northwest. When Beth pitched the idea of buying Hattie's and moving back East, Jasper wasn't so sure.

"I'd been on the high-end (culinary) track and wasn't sure

I'd be happy in a more down-tempo fried chicken joint," he said. But the young couple put their reservations aside and jumped in. They sold their home in Seattle, and in the early 2000s packed up their six-month-old daughter and moved back to their old stomping grounds.

Stepping into an operation with such a powerful historical and cultural tradition wasn't always easy. A lot of Hattie's recipes weren't written down, so Jasper learned them from the long-time kitchen staffers and customers. He took the time, using "oral and visual cues" from customers and cooks to keep Hattie's menu alive. The fried chicken stayed the same. The collard greens didn't change. The salad dressing was made the way Hattie made it. The pecan pie got a few small tweaks but tasted as good as Hattie used to make. Although Jasper had never met Hattie, he wanted to make sure anything he did—from paying his people well to feeding hungry people who couldn't pay—would have pleased her. His customers kept him honest. When he took chicken livers with caramelized onions and bacon off the menu, so many longtime customers complained that he put them back "on secret." It doesn't appear on the menu, but you can get the dish if you ask for it.

As he mastered her dishes, Jasper added some of his own touches, like macaroni and cheese, chicken and dumplings, and ribs. Quickly he realized that owning and running Hattie's wasn't like owning and running just *any* restaurant. Hattie's was an institution. It meant something to the community and the people. It was where people from all walks of life could gather and tuck into a great meal, shoulder-to-shoulder.

"I realized that something I'd been missing in Seattle was having a restaurant with a real sense of purpose and history," he told me later.

But under Jasper and Beth, Hattie's also had a future. In 2010, they opened a Track Shack at the Saratoga Race Course and another Hattie's Chicken Shack near the Wilton Mall. It caters to the performers at the Saratoga Performing Arts Center, and its annual Mardi Gras event has raised over $650,000 for charities since 2001.

## A NEW PLAN

After mulling over my proposition, the Alexanders called the next day. They had a proposition of their own.

"Why don't you buy the whole thing?" Jasper said.

"The whole thing?"

"Yeah. Hattie's in Saratoga Springs. The Hattie's at the track. The Hattie's Chicken Shack out by the mall."

They explained they were hoping to retire in the next decade and loved the idea I pitched. They said they'd taken Hattie's as far as they could but weren't interested in selling to just any buyer. Being the owner of Hattie's carried with it certain responsibilities. You had to remain true to Hattie's legacy. They felt I would do that.

Things moved along pretty quickly after that. We bought Hattie's three restaurants, closed on Lombardo's, and started making plans to refurbish Lombardo's and open a new Hattie's. What's more, we offered Jasper and Beth an employment agreement, and they joined the BFG staff as full-time hospitality experts. They keep Hattie's staffed, run our first business, the Bread Basket Bakery, and oversee the Lombardo's renovation in preparation for reopening as a Hattie's. Boom, boom, and boom. If what we imagine comes true, Lombardo's will become the same draw it was years ago when people came downtown for a concert or a show and would stop in for dinner. It's going to have a New Orleans vibe, more fitting to the decor and the neighborhood. The food will be fantastic.

But our plan doesn't end there. Once Hattie's is up and running in Albany, we want to expand across the country. We see a Hattie's in Detroit. We see one in Watts. We see them popping up in inner cities around the country, doing for those communities what Hattie's has been doing for us for decades—creating good jobs, revitalizing neighborhoods, and setting an example of what generosity, compassion, and goodwill looks like. And all those profits go to charity. If I can prove the model works, perhaps I can get funding from someone like MacKenzie Scott to expand it around the country. We wouldn't make a nickel off it, but how many old buildings can we save? How many streets can we bring back to life with commerce? How many neighborhoods can we bring back to life with our investments, improvements, and good-paying jobs? It's a franchise not only for great food but for social good.

Our plan in Albany is to have people pay what they can afford. Same meals, same service, but if you need a break on your bill, we'll give it to you. Studies show that people that can afford a great meal will pay a little more if they know the surplus is going to help those that are poor and hungry.

Will it work? We'll find out. Who knows? We'll figure it out. Remember, we're getting good at changing the tires on a moving vehicle.

For now, we're scrambling to get the Albany location opened. We've got a lot of work to do. It's an old building, so we're installing new kitchen equipment, signage, and tables. We are rebranding the business and launching a new website with the help of an all-Black advertising firm we hired in Atlanta. When we open, we'll have a big event and use it as a fundraiser for one of our local charities.

## LET'S BUY A BAKERY

As I mentioned earlier, Hattie's is just one of the businesses that BFG started with the goal of raising money for charity and providing good jobs and benefits for talented people.

Our first foray into this area was the Bread Basket Bakery, which Lisa and I bought in 2020. At the time, we had just sold Fingerpaint, and I was starting to think about what I would do after the deal was completed and I had more time on my hands. I wasn't necessarily interested in owning a bakery, but I loved the building the bakery was in and I thought it might make a good investment. It was in an ideal location—right across the street from Congress Park and just a block from the Saratoga Springs History Museum. I'd buy the building, renovate, and keep the forty-year-old bakery as tenants.

It turned out that the building owner was the same person who owned the bakery. She was a very sweet older woman. I met with her and asked if she was interested in selling the building. As a family-run business with narrow margins, they'd never had the resources to upgrade the facilities with new equipment, display cases, and interior updates. The building had wonderful character but needed to be refreshed a bit. If she sold me the building, I would do everything for her and allow her to focus on running her business. She smiled. It was a tired smile. She was in her seventies and had been getting up at 3:30 in the morning for forty years. She was ready to retire, she said. Was I interested in buying both the bakery and the building?

Own a bakery? Now it was my turn to smile. I can't boil water, let alone knead a loaf of dough or bake a muffin. But as I looked around the busy bakery and watched staff members taking orders, making sandwiches, and brewing coffee, I got the sense that they knew what they were doing. I asked her about her succession plan. Did she have managers who could take over for her? Did she have experienced employees who could help maintain the quality of her products and service? I had no idea how much a place like this would make in a year, but it seemed busy and profitable. I started to warm up to the idea. Also, I liked the idea of being able to stop in when I was downtown and get a free blueberry muffin. I pictured myself walking into a crowded bakery and everyone looking up and shouting "Ed!" the way the patrons in "Cheers" would greet Norm. What's not to like about that arrangement? I said, "I like the idea. But I need to talk to my wife first."

Lisa thought I was crazy. She's much more practical than

I am. Also, she was aware that the "details" of running a bakery would likely fall to her.

"What do we know about running a bakery?" she said when I unveiled my grand scheme. Staffing, vendors, insurance, benefits, payroll...

"How hard can it be?" I said. "We've got people on staff who know the work. We'll raise money for charity. We'll give away free cookies to kids who get a good report card."

Needless to say, Lisa was right. Running a bakery *is* hard. But we followed through on the plan: We bought the building, renovated it, and gave the staff pay increases and health insurance. We even added a second satellite location. We kept the bakery's original logo but gave it a new website and added the catchline: "Bread Basket Bakery. Baking a difference." We added our BFG logo and made it clear that our profits would go directly to local charities working to end hunger and food insecurity.

I'm not going to pretend that owning and operating a bakery was easy, but I will say all the work was worth it. The renovations took longer than expected, and there was some staff turnover, but now that we're up and running in two locations, we're starting to see some light at the end of the tunnel. We hired a general manager with experience in both fine and casual dining. We also have a head cake artist who has a degree in baking, production, and management and has worked at the Bread Basket for years. When Jasper and Beth sold Hattie's and joined our staff, they began overseeing operations at the bakery.

## VOORHEESVILLE

We're still expanding our restaurant operations. In 2022, Lisa and I bought three decrepit buildings on Main Street in downtown Voorheesville, my hometown, and we plan to open a sports tavern and a cafe catering to the cyclists using the nearby Albany County Helderberg-Hudson Rail Trail. We're going to donate all profits to youth sports.

Voorheesville has only 3,000 people, and over the years, its downtown area has lost some businesses and doesn't have the vigor it had when I was growing up there. In 2021, we held a community event to explain the project and get feedback from residents. It was a cold, rainy day, but over 300 people turned out and completed questionnaires and told us what they'd like to see built. Our final proposal reflected what they asked for.

The plan is to raze the three buildings and build a 5,500-square-foot tavern and a two-story cafe with affordable apartments on the top floor. The proposal we gave the Planning Commission showed how the new construction would "harmonize with the history" of the downtown area and maintain its Victorian feel. We hope the project brings new life to the downtown and sparks other investment.

And it's a fun project. I graduated from Clayton A. Bouton High School in Voorheesville, and it feels great to be building something to help the community and help local athletes. It also gets our entrepreneurial juices flowing.

# CHAPTER 7

# YOU WILL STEP IN IT

It's no secret that white people have difficulty talking about race. The book *White Fragility* talks about this. Most white people live their entire lives without meaningful interaction with people of color, particularly Black people. As a result, most white people don't realize or acknowledge all the privileges we've enjoyed. We grow up thinking we're entitled to what we have and that everyone should treat us like we're special. No one's challenged the beliefs we're raised with—that America is a white country, white people shaped our economic and political masterpieces, and that all our cultural and artistic brilliance is defined by white people.

We're pretty proud of ourselves, and we never get pushed out of our racial comfort zone. It's inconceivable to us that a minor traffic stop would result in us getting shot or that someone might call the cops on us because we're sitting in a coffee shop waiting for our friends. So when someone comes along and knocks us off our pedestals, we freak out. When someone tells us we shouldn't use a term we've used all our lives—like "being sold down the river" or "no comments from the peanut gallery"—we get all bent out of shape. *What do you mean that's racist?* We scoff. We get defensive. We dismiss their concerns as petty or insignificant. Or we shut down and don't say anything. What do you mean I can't have a *master bedroom* in my house? You're offended that I said *cakewalk*?

I'm bringing this up for a couple of reasons.

First, it's true. Our language is loaded with racist terms, and people like you and me must get off our high horses and watch what we say. Some terms or phrases are insensitive and hurtful, and we have to quit using them. Moreover, we must say something when we hear others using them. Remember how Trump said that his impeachment inquiry was a "lynching"? If you were a Black person, how would that make you feel? Tens of thousands of Black people in this country were tortured, burned alive, and hung from trees, often as crowds of white people gathered to watch. White people would buy postcards of these lynchings and send them to relatives around the country (until the US postmaster finally announced he would no longer deliver them). This is the horror that Black people lived with for decades in the Jim Crow South. So when a privileged white racist like Trump compares his ridiculous political problems to the terror of living as a Black person in the post-bellum, it's demeaning and incredibly insensitive.

But it's common. Remember that white Republican from Georgia who called Obama "uppity"? Or the Kentucky Congressman speaking at a GOP dinner who said of Obama,

"That boy's finger does not need to be on the button." Don't think for a second that those terms were harmless barbs. They were like racist bullets being fired by ignorant, insensitive white idiots.

The second reason I bring this up: I don't want anyone to think the risk of misspeaking is a good reason to avoid the work I'm promoting in this book. Don't let your fear of inadvertently using a racist or racially insensitive term be an excuse to sit on the sidelines. The kind of work I'm talking about will require that you move out of your comfort zone, talk to people you've never talked to before, and learn to communicate better. You're probably going to step in it a few times. You're probably going to piss a few people off. You'll try the patience of the people you're working with. But you have to learn from your mistakes.

I know I have.

## I DIDN'T MEAN IT THAT WAY

I was giving a speech to the United Way last year, not long after we started our foundation. There were about a hundred people there, including scores of people who live and work in some of the rough neighborhoods where our projects are located. Many were people of color I recognized from working with Norma and Jamil from Frank Chapman, and Corey Ellis from the Black Chamber of Commerce. I talked about how I hoped our projects at the Frank Chapman Memorial Institute, Lombardo's Restaurant, and some other places would spur additional development from other groups in Albany's rough neighborhoods.

"You drive through some of these inner-city neighborhoods now, and they're in such disrepair," I said. "You drive down a block, and a half-dozen of the buildings are vacant or condemned, and the only businesses are a barber shop, a liquor store, and a place that sells lottery tickets. There's nothing there. We hope our projects will bring in more businesses and improve these neighborhoods."

It wasn't long before word got back to me that I'd fucked up in a big way. Instead of getting people excited about the prospects of urban renewal, all I did was piss them off. They were offended. Here comes the rich white guy from the posh community of Saratoga Springs telling us how rundown our neighborhoods are and how he will fix them. It wasn't long before people who weren't even at the speech came up to me, saying, "Hey, I hear you really stepped in it at the United Way." People called Jah. "I hear your boss fucked up big time. What's his problem?" Of course, the *last* thing I wanted to do was offend anyone. I wanted to inspire them, and I'd failed miserably. All I could do was reach out to as many people as I could and personally apologize. Talk about stepping in it. That was a steaming pile.

On another occasion, I met some folks at the University Club to show them the renovations and discuss the timetable for when the work would be finished. I met Jah and Stephanie, our project manager, and we greeted a couple of the local chamber leaders and the new chief executive officer, who'd just been hired. She introduced herself to me.

"Deshanna," she replied. "Deshanna Wiggins."

Our leader, Jahkeen Hoke, with Deshanna Wiggins of the Albany Black Chamber of Commerce.
(Photo Credit: Tyeisha Ford)

"Deshanna," I said, shaking her hand. I was eager to show her that I was just a regular guy and not some aloof, prim, and proper white guy. So I thought I'd joke around with her a bit.

"Deshanna," I said, musing. "Why can't anybody have a normal name like Bob or Sue or Joe anymore?"

As she withdrew her hand, she cocked her head slightly and smiled at me.

"Well, Ed, it *is* a normal name," she said, laughing. "It's just not normal to you."

Deshanna handled my idiotic comment with a lot of grace, but later I kicked myself. I felt like an asshole. I'd tried to joke with her and start building a bond, but instead I'd made myself look like an ass. I'd stepped in it again.

## ACTIONS MEAN SOMETHING

When we donated a million dollars to the survivors of the Tulsa Massacre, I conferred with Jah on the plane. I knew I'd be giving remarks at a press conference, and I wanted to choose my words carefully.

For example, I originally planned to say that I was angry about how these survivors had been stonewalled for years by politicians who refused to compensate them for what they'd endured.

"I wouldn't say 'stonewall'," Jah advised.

"No?" There was no question the courts and the government had been stonewalling these people. They'd been denied justice for decades.

"'Stonewall' was the nickname for a celebrated Confederal general," Jah explained. General Thomas Jackson got the nickname for the way he stood up to Union attacks. According to his biographer, Jackson was a slave owner who likely believed God had sanctioned slavery and that "man had no moral right to challenge its existence."

I had no idea that term might be considered culturally insensitive. (It's also insensitive to the LGBTQ community because of the 1969 Stonewall Riots in New York City when police raided the Stonewall Inn gay club.)

So, instead of accusing Oklahoma of stonewalling the Tulsa survivors, I said I was angry that the state was "running out the clock" on them, which probably had more power because these survivors were all over a hundred years old and one of them was 108.

## LEARN FROM YOUR MISTAKES

The point here is that it's okay to make mistakes as long as you learn from them. After you step in it a few times, you start to look at language differently. You learn to avoid terms like "grandfathered in" (a term adopted by seven Southern states during Reconstruction to prevent Black people from voting), "lynch mob," and "cakewalk," which was a dance performed by enslaved Black people for the entertainment of plantation owners. You learn to steer clear of terms like "black mark" and "blackballed," in which black is used to describe something wrong and is subconsciously racial in nature.

I'm not saying this is easy. I'm a plain-spoken guy. I'm blunt, frankly, and I appreciate direct language. Years ago, you might say I liked to "call a spade a spade," which for half a millennium meant "tell it like it is." But I won't use that term anymore, for reasons that are obvious to me now but weren't five years ago. I don't care if it's been in the language since 120 AD. If it's polarizing, avoid it. If people are offended, they'll stop listening to you, and you'll get nowhere.

Luckily, the Black people I work with have been patient and helpful as I've learned to get my language right. I was talking about this learning process recently with Kathleen McLean, a Black consultant with a focus on equity, team building, and leadership development. She's a brilliant woman, a real leader. I mentioned how embarrassed I'd been after the United Way speech, but Kathleen was reassuring.

"Ed, your actions speak louder than words," she said. "If anyone wants to suggest that you're insensitive, those of us in the Black community will have your back.

"To do the work you do requires an internal drive," she said. "Anyone who gets to know you can see that your whole body is connected to this work. White people need to start a journey to understand how they are silently complicit in perpetuating racism in this country, and you are already on that journey."

Kathleen continues to coach me. After my Chamber acceptance speech, where I encouraged that banquet hall crammed with wealthy white people to patronize Black businesses, Kathleen mentioned how important those comments were. I agreed. They can hire Black businesses out of the goodness of their hearts, I said, but there are even better reasons. Businesses owned by people of color can bring a higher level of service or a more competitive price, or a creative twist you may not see in white competitors.

"They might surprise you," I said.

"I love what you're saying, Ed," she replied. "White businesses are missing an opportunity by not using these talented business owners like Kizzy Williams or Marie Campbell. But to say they will be 'surprised' reinforces a prevailing bias that these businesses are not quite as good as the white ones, doesn't it?"

And, of course, she was right.


## TAKE YOUR TIME

Jah has been a vital part of helping me through this minefield of racist language. Right after we started BFG, he cleaned up the mess I made at Frank Chapman when I walked into a meeting with Norma Chapman and Jamil Hood and said I wanted to buy their building for a dollar so I could spend another $500,000 to fix it up. If Jah had been around that day, he would have held up both hands and said, "Slow down, Ed. Do you think they are going to *give* you the thing they've fought their whole life for? How do you think they'll feel about you coming in and telling them their place is a wreck?" Well, luckily, Jah was able to smooth that one over for me, and the Frank Chapman center got fixed, and Jamil and Norma became my good friends.

Nowadays, Jah and I have some pretty frank discussions about what I can say and what I shouldn't say. I lean on him. He lets me.

"You need a confidential consultant, a go-to," he told me once. "Anyone in your position needs that. You need someone in the car with you, someone you can talk to and ask, 'How do I navigate this?'"

He's advised me not to go into discussions acting confident or appearing ego-driven or naïve enough to tell people they can be successful if they do things my way. I've been successful, and I know how to get things done, so why not follow my lead? Well, because it doesn't work that way. The people you're helping aren't the same as you. They haven't had what you've had. It's not so easy for them.

"You're dealing with people who are motivated by different things," Jah once told me. "African Americans, Latinos—they're social first. Trust has never been built in or granted to them, so the only way you can build that trust and credibility is with time and patience and getting to know them. You can't be driving an agenda, man."

Coming back from Tulsa, he told me our greatest gesture was not giving the survivors a million dollars. It was the fact that we went there. We saw them. We saw what they went through. We saw their tragedy, and we listened to them. And *then* we gave them a gift. But the thing the survivors talked about was how this man came all the way from New York to meet them and talk to them and shake their hands.

You have to understand that many people in the Black community are afraid to be successful. They fear success because they're afraid someone will take it away from them. White people have done that throughout history. We promised former slaves forty acres and a mule, and all they got was Jim Crow and another hundred years of enslavement. So the second they see a white man coming in hot with an agenda, they back off. *What's this guy* really *after? At what point is he going to break* this *promise?*

It was like that in Albany when we first started doing projects. Before we went out there and showed people who we are, they were always pulling Jah aside and asking him, "What's this Mitzen guy's game? Why's he doing this? White guys just don't do shit for free, so this guy's got to have some angle. What is it?"

Another thing to remember about stepping in it: People of color are used to how clueless we are about race. Nothing shocks or surprises them anymore. This isn't a reason for those reading this book to be lazy or careless, but it is a good reason to put yourself out there. You have to take the risk. Standing silently off to the side does nothing to challenge the power and privilege we need to tear down in this country. When you screw up, admit it and accept the criticism.

Some people will get angry with you, and you can't blame

them. People of color have been putting up with our lame-ass ignorance and bullshit for generations; they've got a right to be impatient with us. But many will cut you some slack and patiently explain why what you just said was offensive. Listen to them. Just as racist behaviors can be learned, so can antiracist ones. It takes time and it takes a commitment on your part.

## TALKING ABOUT RACE

Many white people have a hard time simply conversing with a person of color. Psychologists call it "racial anxiety." While Black people may be concerned about facing discrimination and hostility, white people worry that people of color will assume they're racist. Many white people become self-conscious and nervous, worried they'll say something stupid that will only *confirm* that they are racist. As a result, they avoid saying anything, or else they tighten up and act nervous. They avoid eye contact. They speak fast. Their voice gets slightly choked or comes out pitched higher than normal. Researchers have studied this phenomenon. In one study of patients of color seeing doctors from other races, researchers found that the patients have shorter visits and more often report stiff, unpleasant reactions with their doctor than do white patients.

Conversations about race can also test friendships between white people and Black people. My Black friend Rosalind told me how she broke off her friendship with a white woman after the woman objected to Roz's social media posts about race. Her white friend said the posts made her feel "uncomfortable" and were insulting in light of how close the two of them were. "I'm sorry you're experiencing momentary unease," Roz said. "But Blacks have been handcuffed and knocked down by whites for centuries. Maybe you need to get over yourself?"

Robin DiAngelo, the author of *White Fragility*, calls this racism "by a thousand cuts."

"It's the well-meaning white people at the overwhelmingly white workplace that send Black people home exhausted and wondering if it's worth discussing racism as all," DiAngelo told CNN. "There's a question I've asked people of color for twenty years: How often have you attempted to give a white person—who thinks they're open-minded and sensitive to racism—feedback on their inevitable and often unintentional, but hurtful, racist assumptions and behaviors—and had that go well for you? The number one answer to that question? *Never.*"

Here's my takeaway from all this: If you're a white person who wants to be part of the solution and not part of the problem, don't try to pretend you're "woke" or somehow different from all the other white people. You're not. You probably have no idea how good you've had it. You were born into a caste system that put you in the top tiers. You grew up learning that it's better to be white. Racism isn't always deliberate and purposely mean-spirited. We white people can be pretty fucking condescending.

All you can do is take risks and learn from your mistakes. Engage. When you get called out, don't use it as an excuse to withdraw and say, "Well fuck this. I'm not going to say anything." You're going to feel defensive, but you've got to fight that feeling so you can continue to grow.

Kathleen calls it going on a journey. You make progress in small increments, and you have to challenge yourself within. Ask yourself, *What do I want my legacy to be?* She does this exercise where people get six cards and they have to write down thirty-two values that are important to them. She sets a timer and people jot down things like *fun, friendship, wisdom, reputation, memories,* and so forth. Then she asks them to pick their top six. Again, there's a timer, so people can't overthink what's important to them. Finally, she tells them to pick their top two.

Without fail, the two most important values are *leaving a legacy* and *family.*

"And so, when your grandchildren say to you, 'What did you do when George Floyd died?' what do you want to be able to say to them? That you went fishing in your boat or hosted a party at your vacation home? The answer you give to that question will drive your journey toward understanding racism."

Listening to Kathleen, I couldn't help but think of my daughter. Grace came to work for the foundation last year, and earlier in the day I'd run into her at Kizzy Williams' restaurant. She was there to take pictures of Kizzy, and Kizzy greeted her with a big hug like she's part of the family. Grace has always been socially conscious, but I don't think she always saw me as being that way. I think that's changing. I think it's good for her to see the work I'm doing and to join me in that work. For me, it's great to think that Grace is there to carry on this work.

That's our journey.

# CHAPTER 8

# THE SLANTED PLAYING FIELD

We met Patrick LaFortune outside the Albany training center on Broad Street. The industrial building had been damaged in a flood and was gutted, and Patrick was watching a group of young Black kids pour cement and run a screed across the top to repair a damaged ramp.

"Put some pressure on it," he told the teenagers. "Pull that straight edge back and forth, back and forth."

LaFortune owns a home renovation business, but in his spare time, he runs a pre-apprenticeship program that helps his students become masons, pipe fitters, electricians, iron-workers, and carpenters. He teaches them all the basic stuff, they figure out what work they like best, and they move on to become apprentices in the building trades. BFG gave the program $200,000 to pay for materials.

"These kids come to us a little rough around the edges," Patrick says as he guides us through the old warehouse, where students have studded out walls for classrooms and workshops. You can still see the penciled fractions where they calculated the doorway headers. When they get good enough to qualify for union jobs, they stand to make $60,000 or so in the workforce.

That's a big deal for the dozens of young people—most of them Black. And it helps in the trades, where there's a shortage of skilled workers, and there isn't much diversity. But when you think about how far behind these kids and their families are financially, you realize that this is a pretty small step. Getting more forgotten teenagers into the trades will help, but it's just the beginning.

## A BROAD CHASM

There is a huge wealth gap between white people and people of color in this country. And I'm not talking just about those who may have dropped out of school. Black people with college degrees are way behind white graduates. Black college graduates have less wealth and earn less money than white people who *didn't* go to college.

The median wealth of Black people is under $20,000 a year, while for white people it's over $170,000. When you look at savings and home equity and other forms of wealth, they own about a tenth of what white families have. They don't have rainy day funds to pay for emergencies. They have measly retirement savings. They have little family wealth to pass along to their children.

And this has been going on for generations. After nearly 250 years of slavery, it continued with Jim Crow, when freed slaves were enslaved a second time by sharecropping, segregation, and outright intimidation that kept them in the fields and working on plantations. And it continued when they fled north in the Great Migration, when they were funneled into segregated neighborhoods in New York, Chicago, Los Angeles, and everywhere in between. They were forced to live in shitty walkups, and they paid more in rent than white tenants because the Black tenants had fewer choices. They were denied access to hospitals. Banks wouldn't loan them money to buy real estate. If they could get loans, they paid higher interest rates, and their property didn't grow in value the way a white family's would. If you were a Black woman, the only work you could find in most northern cities were the jobs no one else wanted—washing clothes, scrubbing toilets, and cleaning houses. Even into the 1950s, Black women working in New York or Chicago as domestics earned about as much as they had picking cotton in the South. The disparity continues today. Overall, women earn eighty-three cents for every dollar a white man earns, and Black women earn just sixty-four cents.

The wealth gap for Black people trickles down into every financial pore. Despite anti-discrimination laws, their unemployment is almost twice what it is for white people, and white people get more callbacks for job applications. Poor Black people carry less debt, but their debt payments are twice as costly as a white person with a credit card or mortgage. Since they live in old, leaky, rented homes, their energy bills are higher. They're exposed more often to lead paint and mold. They're more likely to live near deadly environments, like toxic dumps or polluted industrial zones.

Their landlords either don't give a shit or have no financial incentive to improve the properties they rent to others.

Believe it or not, I know what that life is like. In college, all I could afford was a drafty old walkup. In the winter, the ratty curtains would puff out when the wind blew through the rotten siding. When I'd come home at night, I'd stomp on the kitchen floor and wait for a few seconds before turning on the lights. This would give the cockroaches some time to find their hiding places so I could pretend the place wasn't infested. That apartment was a shithole, but for me, it was temporary. My family wasn't rich, but I knew I'd eventually get out. My Black neighbors would never get out.

## IT GETS WORSE

Discrimination is alive and well in the workplace. Black people often can't get jobs that offer pensions and 401(k) accounts. About half as many Black people have retirement savings plans—401(k)s or IRAs—as white people. If you're Black and you have a retirement account, it's probably one-third the size of a white person's. It's hard to save when you're paying too much in rent, your debt payments have a higher interest rate, and your family has no money to pass down or loan to you.

The Great Recession from 2007 to 2009 only made it worse. Most white people came back from their losses. Black people didn't. White wealth grew about 15 percent from 2008 to 2016. Black wealth dropped by a third.

We saw it again during the pandemic. Minorities make up the bulk of labor jobs in this country, the jobs you can't do from home. They have to show up at work, and when work is closed, they're in deep shit. They have to eat into their savings, collect unemployment, and then find new jobs when the world reopens. While white people were happily buying low-priced stocks when the market fell, building even more wealth, African Americans could only watch as what little they had saved dwindled further.

How would that make *you* feel? You've been knocked back so many times, you have to wonder if it's even worth trying anymore. Jah talks about this. If ambition runs at 200 miles per hour like a Formula 1 race car, why, as a Black person in this country, would you ever climb above 60? What good would it do?

## NO HELP FROM THE GOVERNMENT

The federal government often made things worse for Black people and Hispanics. Social Security excluded agricultural workers and domestic servants, who were predominantly African American, Hispanic, and Asian. Early union laws excluded nonwhites. From 1934 to 1962, $120 billion in new housing subsidized by the government largely went to white families. Nonwhite families got less than 2 percent. The Supreme Court outlawed restrictive covenants that barred homeowners from selling or renting homes to African Americans, but the practice continued for decades. Banks used federal guidelines to base appraisals on race, devaluing Black homes and charging more for loans. Economists, meanwhile, shrugged and said segregation was "market-driven."

In the 1950s and '60s, as the white people fled to the suburbs, the federal government subsidized the boom and built major freeways to accommodate the sprawl. These "renewal" projects often ran straight through African American communities, creating blight. We saw this in Albany, and we saw it in Tulsa, but the crime was repeated in dozens of cities.

Are these past crimes just history? No. They all contributed to today's tremendous wealth gap. As housing prices soared, white people grew rich off their unfair historic advantage. They continue to benefit. And they pass it down to their children. Our history put people of color so far behind that they will never catch up unless, as a country, we focus for an extended time on fixing it.

## WHAT YOU CAN DO

As a well-off white person, you probably have some juice in your community or your state. Maybe you have some clout on the national level.

Whatever the case, you have an obligation to see the world for what it is. Starting in colonial times, our country was built on the backs of slaves. Even after we freed them, we continued to use them. As our country grew and enriched itself, we continually gave them the shitty end of the stick.

To justify all this, we've allowed a certain mythology to invade our sensibilities. We want to believe that higher education is the "great equalizer"—that if we can get more Black people graduating from college that the wealth gap will shrink. We've also convinced ourselves that Black parents don't emphasize education enough. We want to believe that if we can help Black people buy homes or build more Black-owned banks or teach them "financial literacy," we'll be all good. We want to believe African American problems are a result of too many single-parent families or that Black people need to emulate Asians' or Koreans' savvy entrepreneurship. If we can just get them to open more businesses, they can pull themselves up. If we can get them to save more.

I hear this kind of stuff all the time. It's bullshit.

Black college grads are 30 percent poorer than white college grads. When the race starts, the white horses are already to the first turn when the Black ones come out of the gate. And they can't close the gap; white households with an employed breadwinner earn ten times what a Black household earns. Even when the white breadwinner is unemployed, the white household has a higher net wealth than the African American family whose main breadwinner has a job. Think about that for a minute. What is going on here?

This must be because Black families don't support education, right? No. Studies show that African American families tend to be *more supportive* than white families when it comes to their children's education. They value it. They don't take it for granted.

When it comes to home ownership, the government made it (and our system continues to make it) profoundly difficult for Black people to gain wealth through that route. Nothing new there. African American GIs coming home from World War II typically didn't bother to apply for home loans because they knew the Veterans Administration would turn them down. Today, banks have a variety of ways to reject mortgage applications from Black people: the homes don't appraise high enough, the applicant has an insufficient down payment, or their debt-to-income ratio is too low.

## MORE MYTHS

Here are a few more truths that white people have to accept:

- Black banks investing in black communities will not turn things around themselves. Expecting black capitalism to solve the problem is just a way to take the problem off the government's back. Black banks just aren't big enough and don't have sufficient access to capital to turn this around themselves. Their patrons don't have much money to save, remember? The assets of the five largest Black-owned banks in the county amount to 1.1 percent of J.P Morgan's assets alone. This is another place where guys like me can step in. Let's use our wealth to give Black entrepreneurs access to the capital they need. We don't have to give it away. We can loan it and offer favorable terms. We can deposit our money in Black-owned banks and work with them to invest. Despite prevailing myths, Black families actually have a higher savings rate than white families. Put your money to work to help close the wealth gap.
- Black entrepreneurship alone is not enough to close the wealth gap. They're just too far behind. White small businesses account for nearly 90 percent of overall sales in the US. Black business accounts for 1.3 percent. You do the math. We need to move that needle, but we must be realistic about how big the impact will be.

- Insanely rich Black celebrities and athletes are anomalies. People like to see the rise of wealthy Black people like Oprah or Michael Jordan or Jay-Z as a sign of Black ascendancy. They aren't. And even the richest Black man in the world—Alike Dangote of Nigeria—is only worth about 5 percent of the richest white man (Bernard Arnault, as of January 2023).
- Many blame the wealth gap on the increasing number of Black single-parent households. Get off that. This notion of Black single moms is the worst kind of racial stereotype. The percentage of two-parent households is indeed higher for white people, but there's a reason for that. Several reasons. Black men are incarcerated at five times the rate of white men. One in eight is in state prison. Black men die of heart disease, cancer, and homicide at much higher rates than white men. One in five Black people dies earlier than if they were white. Studies show that there are more single Black mothers because there are fewer marriageable Black men.

Ironically, Black culture in America is one of our country's most lucrative exports, but African Americans haven't benefited much from it. We export clothing, jewelry, humor, literature, films, and music, a lot of it spawned by the Black struggle in our history. Black artists brought us blues, jazz, rock, funk, gospel, hip-hop, and R&B. Problem is that corporations and record labels haven't done much to include Black people in their business and share in the profits.

## ACCEPT THE REALITY

So, what are you supposed to do? I don't have a secret recipe, but the first step is understanding reality. The playing field is not level. White people like us had so many unfair advantages. Our dads got help from the government while that same government was holding down our Black neighbors. We built wealth in the suburbs at the expense of the Black neighborhoods destroyed by "urban renewal." We got cheap loans, better jobs, union pay, and retirement benefits. We built great businesses because we had unfair access to money.

Are you OK with all that? I'm not.

So here's what I'm going to tell my elected leaders:

- I want you to support community development financial institutions—those banks, credit unions, and other smaller institutes that support small businesses and affordable housing. CDFIs are one way to help Black people purchase homes.
- I want any community that gets block grants from the federal Housing and Urban Development to actively document its actions to promote fair housing. Obama demanded this, but Trump rolled back this requirement. President Joe Biden has directed HUD to fight discriminatory housing practices that continue despite the fifty-year-old Fair Housing Act.
- I want you to support Biden's plan to boost federal contracting with small, disadvantaged businesses by 50 percent. It could inject $100 billion into minority-owned businesses over the next four years.
- Do something to make rental housing more affordable so people of color can save money for a down payment on

a house. Why don't we have a federal renter's tax credit similar to the mortgage interest deduction?

- Make it easier for African American students to afford college. Too many have to default on loans because they don't get higher-paying jobs, and their families don't have the wealth to help them.
- Let's make the government an "employer of last resort" for Black workers held back by low wages and uncertain jobs. Anyone willing and able to work is guaranteed a job with the government. It could be similar to the Works Progress Administration during the Great Depression. Knowing they have this backstop increases Black's bargaining power on the open market. The Center for American Progress calls it a domestic Marshall Plan.

Is any of this realistic in this political day and age? Fair question. It's hard to imagine two political parties coming together to enact these ideas. But that shouldn't stop us from using whatever influence we have to demand them. The only certain thing is that the current system is broken, and no one will fix it if we don't start talking about it and doing something.

Meanwhile, we must do what we can in our own towns and cities. We need to invest in Black and Brown businesses. We need to provide jobs and benefits. Scholarships. Cash flow assistance. Mentorship. Networking.

And we need to support the work of guys like Patrick LaFortune, the contractor training students for careers in construction.

After a quick tour of the training facility, he went back outside to see how the concrete work was going. It looked good. The wet concrete was flat, and he grabbed a trowel to demonstrate how to smooth the surface. Then he sent the students off for a quick lunch break. Later that day, he would return to his real job—a home he was renovating for a first-time buyer. He wasn't going to get rich flipping houses or volunteering to train new tradespeople, but maybe he'd help close the wealth gap a little before he was done.

"People are always saying, 'Why don't you Black people take care of your properties? Why don't you fix them up nice like the people in the suburbs?'" he said as he put away the tools and rinsed out a portable cement mixer.

"Well, it's because we don't *own* them," he said. The suburbs look nice because people own those homes. If we get a chance to own our buildings, we'll fix them up. You'll see. We just need a chance."

# CHAPTER 9

# WHAT'S NEXT

We had a journalist spend a week with us at BFG. He'd read about the foundation and wanted to write a story about the work we were doing. He wanted to understand our mission and unique approach so he could write what he called "a playbook for others who might want to do the same kind of work." Since one of my goals has always been to convince other rich white people that we need to approach philanthropy differently, I was all in favor of having the guy visit.

We kept him pretty busy. He met with Jah, Connie, Jasper, Beth, and Lisa, sometimes more than once and often for hours. He visited Hattie's, Lombardo's, and both Bread Basket locations. I took him to the Frank Chapman Memorial Institute, and we met with Jamil Hood. He interviewed Kizzy Williams, Maria Gallo, and Marie Campbell, the entrepreneurs we worked with. Lisa took him on a tour of the Mohawk Valley Humane Society and recalled how I took her there on her birthday. "Does my gift have a heartbeat?" she asked me on the drive over. Then we pulled up outside their building and she saw that the building had been named after her. "This is your gift," I said. "We just donated a million dollars."

We took him to the University Club, where he met Corey Ellis and Deshanna Wiggins and toured the new Black Chamber of Commerce. He and I drove over to Voorheesville, met with the mayor, and toured the location where our two restaurants were under construction. We had him over for dinner at the farm, and I showed him the Ferrari we planned to auction off for the YWCA in Troy. He met with Ray and Kim and toured the brownstone we helped them renovate. He met with Catherine Hegeman, the attorney who initially helped us figure out how we could set up the foundation in a way that gave Lisa and me the freedom to buy and start businesses and make gifts, such as the million dollars we gave the Tulsa survivors.

We sat down with Duane Vaughn, the head of Shelters of Saratoga, the homeless services agency that operates rent-free out of our 4,500-square-foot building at Franklin Square in Saratoga Springs. Connie took him through some of the websites we were building for the businesses we own or support. He attended a news conference in Albany where the mayor announced that BFG was donating a million dollars toward a new aquatic facility to replace the shut down Lincoln Park Pool in Arbor Hill and that I was heading up the $10 million capital campaign to get the facility built. Jah showed him the building we want to turn into an affordable housing pilot project. We spent a few hours with Patrick Lafortune, the Black contractor who teaches young people the trades so they can earn apprenticeships and high-paying skilled-labor jobs. We even stuffed him into a tux and took him to the Capital Region Chamber dinner, where Lisa and I were given the Changemaker Award.

Like I said, we kept him busy. For the rest of us, it was a typical week.

When it was over, I gave him a ride to the airport.

"What'd you think?" I asked.

He looked out the window.

"I don't know if I can do it," he said.

"Do what?"

"Adequately describe what you're doing," he said. "Every day is different. Every project is unlike the last one. You're using business as a seed for social change, I get that. But it's like, *Anything goes.* If it helps people, you'll do it. If you have a template, it's got to be made out of raw clay because it's always changing."

"We have changed our approach a few times," I admitted. "We can afford to try new things and see what works best."

He went on like he hadn't heard anything I said. "The people you help all say the same thing: They feel like you're working *with them* and not just giving them a handout and sending them on their way. They feel like they're partners with you, and that makes them feel...I don't know...*confident,* I guess."

He glanced out the window again. He came in hoping for a tidy story to tell, and what he found was a maelstrom of restless activity—restaurants, bakeries, florists, vocational training programs, animal care centers, homeless shelters, dog-sitting services, daycare centers, and downtown renewal projects. He was trying to figure out how to package all that up into a model other people could follow. "It's going to be a challenge," he said. Then he said it three more times before we got to the airport.

"I will tell you one thing for certain, though," he said. "Everyone in your organization is *all in*. Both feet. To a person, they have found their dream job—including you and Lisa."

As I drove home, I thought about what he said. I chuckled. Connie, the marketing head I stole from Madison Square Garden as my second hire for BFG, has a great way of describing our ethos. "We are living what we are becoming," she says. "We're open and flexible in response to what the community needs. We're living, breathing, and growing because that is what will work. It's what our community needs. And the DNA of every community is different. What works here may not work somewhere else."

So, what you do in your community may not look like what we're doing. That's fine. The key is learning what your community needs and finding a solution.

"Our message is that above all else, you have to do *something*," Jah told our visitor that week. "It doesn't have to be what BFG is doing. This is just what *we* needed to do. Someone else, working in another part of the country, will find something else. The important thing is just to *do something* because not enough is being done right now."

## WHAT WE'VE LEARNED

Since we started BFG in 2020, we've discovered a lot about how to do this work. At first glance, it looks like our projects are random and disconnected. But they aren't. When we renovate Lombardo's and open a Hattie's, we expect a cascading effect. We expect the restaurant will draw people downtown like Lombardo's once did. People will grab a meal at Hattie's and then go to a play at the Capital Repertory Theater or the newly renovated Palace Theater, both just down the street on Pearl. We expect some of the nearby abandoned buildings to be converted to apartments or affordable housing, possibly by us. The drug dealers and users accustomed to empty buildings and vacant streets will get uncomfortable and find somewhere else to operate.

"People will see the light coming from Lombardo's again, and they'll think, *Stuff is happening here*," Jah told me the day he first took me around to look at Lombardo's. "And they'll think, *I want to be a part of that.*"

When you're the first to invest in a neglected area like the neighborhood around Lombardo's, some risk is involved. But the investor who follows you has less risk and the investor who follows *that* investor has even less. There's a cascade. It's a gamble being the first investor, but if you want something to happen, you have to be willing to take that chance. You have to be willing to spend the money without a surefire return.

That's what we're willing to do. We're doing it with Lombardo's. We did it with the Wallace Turner Law building. We're doing it with the University Club for the Albany Black Chamber of Commerce.

Everything we do falls under the umbrella of building better communities. That's why we're working with agencies that help battered women, training struggling parents to be better mothers and fathers, and funding programs that bring affordable child care to working families. That's why we're helping inner-city kids learn how to be plumbers, masons, electricians, carpenters, and pipefitters. We need these people. We need them to have great jobs and the incentive to buy into and rebuild their neighborhoods.

This is the ecosystem. It's not a fast fix. But it works. All it takes is for rich white people like Lisa and me to accept the challenge. Think like Andrew Carnegie. Accept your responsibility to society. Get to work.

## GETTING STARTED

Jah's theory is that there are three types of philanthropists: people like me who put themselves out there publicly and aren't afraid to try new things; "quiet" givers who write checks and remain anonymous; and rich people who feel the urge to help but don't know where to start. Whatever group you fall into, let me share some things I've learned in the first years of running BFG.

## LISTEN TO THE PEOPLE

Don't ride in like the noble knight waving a checkbook telling people what you think will work. In other words, don't barge in like I did during my first meeting at Frank Chapman, and start setting an agenda and the terms of how you'll help.

Instead, find out first if they even *want* help, then find out what they need and how they think the problem should be addressed. If they ask for your advice—and they probably will—give it freely. Share your business knowledge and entrepreneurial skills. Utilize your expertise. For example, my background is in marketing. BFG has a highly skilled marketing and communication team. So, in addition to giving grants to budding entrepreneurs, we also help them with their logos, websites, and marketing plans—but only if they want us to.

And when they're up and running, call all your wealthy friends and tell them to patronize these businesses.

## BUILD A GREAT TEAM AROUND YOU

I can't emphasize this enough. When Lisa and I started BFG, we didn't advertise for a CEO to run the organization. Instead, I asked around. I met with people and talked with them about who they thought might be a good fit. I got in touch with Jahkeen Hoke after I read an essay he wrote and asked him to recommend someone. But the more we talked, the more convinced we were that he was perfect for the job. Jah was just as comfortable talking to suits in the boardroom as he was talking to a street vendor in the hood, and he had the drive to make a difference in his hometown of Albany. He had experience with urban renewal and affordable housing. He understood finance. What's more, he knew the players in Albany. He knew who had real juice and who were phoneys.

Likewise, Connie Frances Avila, our chief brand officer, fell into her role with us. She and her husband had fled Manhattan for Saratoga Springs during COVID-19, and we met through a mutual friend. She had experience in marketing sports, entertainment, and media and had worked for Madison Square Garden. She was highly skilled and well-known in her field. She had no nonprofit experience, but I saw that as a plus. I wanted to market BFG differently. Connie understood that if your messages aren't engaging and compelling that people will just move on and ignore you. I wanted to inspire action, and Connie could do that.

For example, when we gave a $500,000 grant to Wellspring, a facility that helps people get out of abusive relationships, Connie wanted to do more than just write a check. So she commissioned an artist to create a series of panels for the entrance to their facility that greets people as they come in. It's called "Seasons," and it depicts a hopeful trajectory of someone's life. It is an unspoken reassurance to Wellspring's clients that they've come to the right place. That's the kind of thoughtfulness and creativity Connie brings to our work.

When we started doing renovations and building projects, Lisa and I knew right away that we'd need a skilled project manager. We found one in Stephanie Marotta-Johnson. She'd worked for several years for a local contractor I know as well as architectural and construction firms. She'd managed the renovation of a historic farmhouse at our farm and had become a workout partner of Lisa's. She'd left the construction business to pursue other interests, but Lisa managed to lure her to BFG. Now she oversees everything—renovating old buildings like Lombardo's and Frank Chapman, and constructing new ones in places like Voorheesville. Frankly, I don't know how she manages everything we throw at her.

Once we had our core, the BFG team grew like wildfire. Jasper and Beth, the former owners of Hattie's, came to work for us to oversee all our restaurants and bakeries. We hired a CFO, an HR director, a marketing director, a property and event coordinator, a bookkeeper, a couple of content creators, and several administrative folks that keep the office humming. We hired chefs and bakers and wait staff for the three Hattie's restaurants.

As you can see, we're not a typical nonprofit. Although all profits go to charity, we are a business operation. We want our restaurants and buildings to be the best they can be, so we hire the best we can find, pay them well, and give everyone benefits.

## FOLLOW YOUR HEART

At BFG, we only get involved in projects that resonate with us. I donated money and signed on to raise funds for the Lincoln Park Pool in Albany because we knew how important the former pool at that location had been to Arbor Hill and the surrounding neighborhood. Jah had swum there as a kid. The original pool had been at that location for a hundred years before it failed, and every summer, the swim lessons were filled to capacity with neighborhood kids who had nowhere else to swim. "You're putting your money where your heart is," Corey Ellis told me the day we donated a million dollars for the pool.

We don't support every cause or every struggling entrepreneur who comes to us. We've had to turn people away. But the people we have chosen to work with have all gone on to give back in their own way. Kizzy is planting orchards and planning community celebrations. Jamil Hood is expanding from basketball camps to baseball camps. The Black chamber is providing workspaces to young African American graphic artists and photographers to help them make connections and grow their businesses. Maria Gallo is already planning out how she'll be putting profits from Nani's Iced Tea back into her community.

## FACE OPPOSITION WITH GRACE

Don't expect all your projects to sail through on a brisk wind. You will face some resistance.

Lisa and I donated money five years ago for a new homeless shelter in Saratoga Springs, and Shelters of Saratoga gets rejected at every location they propose. "We love the idea, just not in our backyard," say the neighbors time and time again. We still haven't built a new shelter, but we're close.

In Voorheesville, a handful of residents protested our plans to rejuvenate the village downtown with a new restaurant and a nearby bike café, even after knowing we would donate all the profit to youth sports programs. One woman complained that the sports tavern would have too many TVs. Seriously.

Even though we were tearing down some abandoned, dilapidated buildings, one neighbor said he worried his property values would decline. A few said they were worried about traffic and parking. But we went through all the proper steps. We held a big gathering with free food to introduce the town to our project. I sat down with nearby restaurants to get their input. I went to every planning commission meeting and responded to every question. Ninety-nine people out of a hundred supported the project, and the town planners approved it.

## TEST YOUR IDEAS

Don't be afraid to go bravely where no nonprofit has gone before. Since your foundation will be funded with your money, you don't have anyone to answer to. Connect the dots. We are helping a Black-owned funeral parlor expand. We're paying expenses so Kizzy Williams can serve free Thanksgiving dinner at Allie B's. We're exploring building a healthcare center in Arbor Hill for a nurse practitioner. We backed an agency, the Baby Institute, which helps adults become better parents. We recently bought them a new twelve-passenger van to help transport mothers and their children. Now, most of that work is quite different from running restaurants, but that doesn't mean we shouldn't be doing them, right? They're part of the ecosystem that makes a community strong.

That said, go forth gently. Take time to measure your effect, and if you aren't satisfied, chalk it up to experience and move on. It's OK if you fail from time to time. The real mistake is in not trying *anything*. Trust your instincts. You likely built your wealth partly on hard work and intuition, so don't hesitate to fall back on those qualities in the nonprofit world.

## THE NEXT BIG IDEA

What's next for BFG? Internally, I know we want to establish some specific processes for working with entrepreneurs. Now that we've worked with several, we have a good idea of what works well and what could work better. Jah wants to build out a process with a defined beginning and end.

The Wallace Turner Law firm, for example, worked extremely well. Ray and Kim have a great office and the credibility that comes with that. But more importantly, they know their shit and do great work. As a result, they are growing and developing a solid reputation in the community. They do most of the legal work for BFG, and I have no qualms about sending more business their way. I know they can handle it and will do great work for their new clients.

We would also like to have a better-defined process for identifying businesses we want to either acquire or otherwise bring into our family of companies. Some of our acquisitions took more effort than we expected. For example, we bought the Bread Basket Bakery when it had no baker and no recipes and a building that had to be remodeled. We had some staff conflicts that had to be worked out. One location doesn't generate the business it needs to. But Jasper and Beth are aware of the situation, and they'll find solutions.

We still have high hopes for taking Hattie's national and establishing it in big cities where the story and the food will resonate. Will Hattie's move on to Atlanta, Chicago, Detroit, Kansas City, and elsewhere? In what form—the older, traditional, full-service sit down like we plan for Albany or the streamlined takeout restaurant we have at the strip mall? We'll see.

## AFFORDABLE HOUSING: CLIMBING THE PYRAMID

One of our next goals is to see if we can get some affordable housing projects going in Albany. That one's a tough nut to crack, but we are optimistic and have experience in that area. Before Jah came to work for us, he did predevelopment work for a $150 million housing project. He managed the property acquisition, planning work, and environmental surveys. He worked with the engineers and architects to design the project. He boiled a three-year process down to eight months through muscle and will.

We see housing as a crucial step in developing the ecosystem. When people can get in a place that gives them "comfort and confidence," great things can happen. We talk about Maslow's hierarchy of needs, a pyramid showing the progressive stages of a human's needs. At the base of the pyramid are physiological needs, like air, water, clothing, and so forth. The second tier of the pyramid represents safety needs, like personal security, employment, health, and property. Once those physiological and safety needs are met, a person can move on to higher-order needs—love and belonging, self-esteem, and self-actualization. Self-actualization is the peak. That's when you experience the desire to be the best you can be. You have the courage and confidence to experiment and innovate.

Before the white people destroyed it, the Greenwood area of Tulsa showed what a Black community could look like when its citizens achieve the upper reaches of that pyramid. Greenwood was the richest community in Oklahoma and one of the most affluent Black communities in the nation. About 100,000 African Americans lived there, and they ran luxury shops, dozens of restaurants, thirty grocery stores, a hospital, a savings and loan, and two newspapers. Greenwood had one of the best school systems in the country. There were two movie theaters and three hotels to accommodate visitors from New York and Chicago. It had its own post office, bus system, and six private airplanes. And remarkably, most residents were only two generations removed from slavery.

When all that was destroyed in just two days in 1921—an incident repeated in those years in many other flourishing Black communities—it ended an accumulation of generational wealth among African Americans. They never recovered and were never given a legitimate second chance. They understood that if they became too successful that white people would tear it down. Their only choice was to throttle back their ambitions and fly low.

So maybe affordable housing can bring back that sense of possibility. Using affordable housing tax credits and other government incentives, BFG could make an investment of a few million dollars to create fifty apartments. We want to create a path to ownership for Black people so they can start building the generational wealth white people have been accumulating for centuries.

In fact, there's an abandoned building across the street from Lombardo's that might fit the bill. There hasn't been any investment on that street in thirty years or more because people packed up and moved to the suburbs. But if we invest with the intentionality of reviving that area, others will follow.

"That could fuel a community," Jah told me one day. "It could be transformational. Fifty families. They need a place to buy groceries. They need restaurants and professional services. If they're comfortable and confident, they can innovate and solve problems. And guess what? There's a thirst for moving into these neighborhoods. The buildings are already there. The live-work spaces are already there. The neighborhoods are already walkable. They're built to be convenient. People will see that, and it will be a momentum-builder."

## THERE'S ALWAYS SOMETHING

Some days I walk into our offices and see all the activity and find it hard to believe how far we've come in such a short time. But quickly, my thoughts turn to all we still have left to do. We've got our work cut out for us.

I remember last year when I first told Lisa I was going to write this book. Our foundation was just a little over a year old, and we were still getting our sea legs. Maybe, Lisa said, we should hold off on a book for a while? Maybe establish more of a track record?

That made good sense, of course. Lisa is the sensible one. But I plunged ahead with the book anyway. I felt a driving need—not to call attention to what we were doing, but to call attention to all the problems crying out to be addressed. My goal was never to brag about what we accomplished. My goal was to motivate people to act.

I'm hoping that telling the story of our foundation gets more rich white guys off their contented asses and getting to work. I don't care if you do it out of guilt or shame or pride, or narcissism. If that's what it takes, then so be it. But I'm telling you, it doesn't have to be that way.

Just do it out of the goodness of your heart.

It's easier that way, and you will never regret it.

# ACKNOWLEDGMENTS

First and foremost, I want to thank the entire staff at Business for Good. Your hard work and dedication to our vision is what makes our work so impactful. None of our successes would have been realities without each of you.

A special shout out to all the wonderful new friends I have made along this journey. It has been an honor to get to know all of you, especially the amazing people in the Capital Region of upstate New York, as well as the loving families in Tulsa, Oklahoma. I would specifically like to mention my phenomenal new legal counsel Raysheea Turner and Kimberly Wallace, as well as Kizzy Williams and her wife Holly from Allie B's Cozy Kitchen; Marie Campbell of Blooms by Marie; John Walker of Kingdom Services; Norma Chapman and Jamil Hood of the Frank Chapman Memorial Institute; Albany leaders Corey Ellis, Tony Gaddy, Deshanna Wiggins, Kathleen McLean, and Mayor Kathy Sheehan; Walter Thorne of the *Albany Business Review*; Maria Gallo of Nani's

Iced Tea; Trent Griffin of Tech Valley Shuttle; and the countless other people that inspire me each and every day.

I'd like to thank my parents. My late father Ed, who showed me how excited you can be by landing a big sponsor for new little league uniforms. And for my mom Carolyn, who encouraged my idea to trick-or-treat for UNICEF when I was five years old.

Finally, I would like to thank my amazing writing partner, Jim Sloan. Jim was instrumental in putting the story together in a way which truly captured the essence of what I'm trying to accomplish in the underserved communities. He has become a trusted confidant and friend as I continue this journey to use business and wealth to raise up those left behind in the American Dream.

# ABOUT THE AUTHOR

**ED MITZEN** is an entrepreneur, business executive, and philanthropist. Before founding Business for Good with his wife, Lisa, he was the founder and CEO of The Fingerpaint Group, a marketing firm with over a billion dollars in valuation.

He grew up in Voorheesville, New York, and earned a bachelor's degree in biology from Syracuse University and an MBA from the University of Rochester's Simon School of Business. Having worked in marketing roles at firms such as Novartis and Cardinal Health, he founded his first company CHS, a marketing consulting firm, at the age of thirty in his basement in Columbus, Ohio. From there, he founded Palio Communications, a healthcare marketing firm acquired by Syneos Health in 2006. In 2008, he founded The Fingerpaint Group, starting on a card table and growing it to over eight hundred employees around the globe and $250 million in annual revenue. The company has been on the Inc. 5000 Fastest Growing Companies list for ten straight years.

His first book, *More Than a Number, the Power of Empathy and Philanthropy in Driving Ad Agency Performance,* was published in 2020. It discusses how compassion for your staff and your communities are actually incredibly good for a company's bottom line success.

Always dedicated to giving back, Ed has sat on numerous non-profit boards, including the Double H Ranch founded by Paul Newman, the NY Capital Region Chamber of Commerce, Union Graduate College, Sunnyview Rehabilitation Hospital, the Saratoga Hospital Foundation, the Saratoga Performing Arts Center, the Hyde Collection art museum, the Waldorf School of Saratoga Springs, New York, and Syracuse University Board of Trustees.

He currently is on the board of the Albany, NY Black Chamber of Commerce.

Ed has three grown children who are his inspiration; Emily (a social worker), Nick (a graphic artist and producer) and Grace (an aspiring writer and photographer). All three live in New York City and the surrounding areas.

Made in United States
North Haven, CT
18 June 2023

37931911R00093